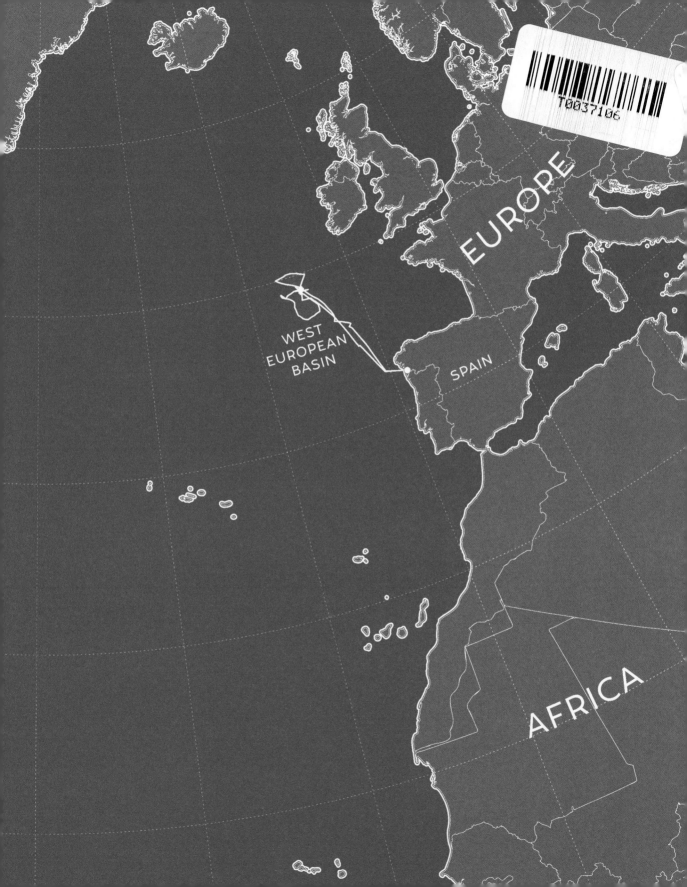

EUROPE

WEST
EUROPEAN
BASIN

SPAIN

AFRICA

A WINDOW INTO THE OCEAN

TWILIGHT ZONE

TWENTY-FOUR DAYS OF SCIENCE AT SEA

MICHELLE CUSOLITO

Charlesbridge

*For Mom and Dad, who raised me
to be open to such adventures*

Text copyright © 2024 by Michelle Cusolito
Photos © by individual copyright holders

Published by Charlesbridge
9 Galen Street
Watertown, MA 02472
(617) 926-0329 • www.charlesbridge.com

Library of Congress Cataloging-in-Publication Data
Names: Cusolito, Michelle, author.
Title: A window into the ocean twilight zone: twenty-four days of science
    at sea / Michelle Cusolito.
Other titles: 24 days of science at sea
Description: Watertown, MA: Charlesbridge, [2024] | Includes
    bibliographical references and index. | Audience: Ages 10 and up |
    Audience: Grades 4-6 | Summary: "Follow a ship full of scientists on
    a voyage to study the deepest part of the sea: the ocean twilight
    zone."—Provided by publisher.
Identifiers: LCCN 2023013057 (print) | LCCN 2023013058 (ebook) |
    ISBN 9781623543020 (hardcover) | ISBN 9781632899422 (ebook)
Subjects: LCSH: Underwater exploration–Juvenile literature. |
    Oceanographic research ships–Juvenile literature. | Oceanographers–
    Juvenile literature.
Classification: LCC GC65 .C874 2024 (print) | LCC GC65 (ebook) |
    DDC 551.46072/3–dc23/eng20230824
LC record available at https://lccn.loc.gov/2023013057
LC ebook record available at https://lccn.loc.gov/2023013058

Printed in China
(hc) 10 9 8 7 6 5 4 3 2 1

Display type set in Double Quick by David Kerkhoff and
    Calderock by Tyfrography
Text type set in Berkeley Oldstyle by URW Software
Printed by 1010 Printing International Limited in Huizhou,
    Guangdong, China
Production supervision by Jennifer Most Delaney
Designed by Diane M. Earley

Title page: *TZEX is tested in the harbor before departure.*

TABLE OF CONTENTS

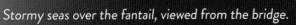
Stormy seas over the fantail, viewed from the bridge.

5:30 PM

THE NORTH ATLANTIC • latitude 48.7° N, longitude 14.7° W

WE KNOW THE STORM IS COMING, but we're still caught off guard by the suddenness of it. The ship lurches to the side. A stool skids across the lab. Another stool crashes to the floor. As the ship rolls in the other direction, we hold on tight to prevent ourselves from falling, too. A pair of sunglasses slides across the counter. A yellow hard hat flies off the top shelf, bounces off the lab table, and hits the linoleum.

Erin yells, "Does anyone have an extra ratchet strap?"

"I do!" I rush out of the lab.

I grip the rails as I walk, my legs set wide apart to keep my balance. Still, I'm tossed side to side on my way up the stairs. I reach my room and brace myself to unlock the closet. I rummage through my belongings, find the bag of bungee cords and ratchet straps, and hurry back to the lab.

I hand the bag to Erin, and she rushes to tie down the bottles and tubes she uses to sample water brought up from deep in the ocean.

Everyone scrambles to secure their equipment. Heidi and John try different methods to protect a bank of computer screens. They finally lay them face down on a rubber mat and use straps to keep them in place. Justin runs extra bungees across a sensitive piece of equipment called a mass spectrometer. Marley and I lay stools on their sides. We gather up loose items such as water bottles, screwdrivers, and pens. We think everything is now well secured, but each new roll of the ship leads to more crashes and reveals additional items we need to strap down.

Later Ken sends a message to the group: "Do take care moving around in your cabin, halls, and common areas to have a hand or two (or three) free to hold railings. Be ready for unexpected rolls. We all want to get to the other side of this storm in good shape!"

We know the weather is going to get worse, but how much worse? And when will we be able to resume the science research we came here to do?

CHAPTER 1

DAYS 1–5

MOBILIZATION

MOVING ONTO THE SHIP

April 29 (Day 1)

VIGO, SPAIN • latitude 42.2° N, longitude 8.7° W

THE BRIGHT RED-AND-WHITE HULL of the Spanish research vessel (R/V) *Sarmiento de Gamboa* stands out among the drabber-looking fishing vessels that crowd the docks. The smell of fish hangs heavy in the air. As members of the science team reach the top of the gangway, crew members wearing hard hats and steel-toed boots take everyone's temperature and squirt a dollop of hand sanitizer into our palms. The team took extraordinary precautions so this research expedition can happen during the Covid-19 global pandemic.

Here on the ship, my roommate is Marley Parker—photographer, videographer, and science communicator. We locate our cabin, drop our giant duffel bags, and claim our bunks. A sign over the toilet in our bathroom says "Do not throw strange objects in the toilet. Only paper." Marley and I chuckle at the funny translation. We're supposed to meet in the mess (dining room) for a safety briefing, but we don't know how to get there. We wander back the way we came and meet a member of the crew who offers to give us a tour before the meeting. By the time he delivers us to the mess, I'm completely turned around and don't know how I'll get back to our room.

Once we finish the safety briefing, it's time to practice what to do if we need to abandon ship. Crew members direct us to our rooms to each grab our red immersion suit (also called a gumby suit) and personal flotation device (also called a PFD or life jacket) and meet back in the designated area. We each lay our immersion suit out on the floor, take off our shoes, and squeeze ourselves into the suit. This can be a complicated process anytime, but keeping my Covid mask properly over my nose and mouth rather than over my eyes is an extra challenge. Postdoctoral Investigator Elena Ceballos Romero giggles as

Marley claims the upper bunk in our room.

L–R: Laetitia, Ken, Helena, Elena, Marley, and me in our gumby suits.

she struggles into her suit, and soon we're all laughing, which only makes the process harder. Zipping up the suit is difficult because my small hands are enclosed in rubber gloves with fingers that are far too long. And I still need to put on my PFD. The whole process probably takes about five minutes, but I keep thinking that I'll have to be faster in an actual emergency. I hope we never need to use this equipment for real.

EXPEDITION GOALS

The team has ambitious goals for this expedition: three ships will meet in the North Atlantic to conduct a variety of complex experiments focused on learning more about the ocean twilight zone. This part of the ocean circles the globe and runs from about 200 meters (656 feet) to 1,000 meters (3,280 feet, about a half mile) below the surface. It receives very little light and is a difficult place to study. It's cold and dark. There's enormous pressure and no clear boundaries, such as sides or a bottom. Everything there is moving. Scientists know more about the surface of the moon than they know about the twilight zone. This expedition seeks to build better estimates about the biomass (the amount of living things), biodiversity (the variety of living things), and food webs in the twilight zone. Scientists also want to understand how carbon moves from the atmosphere to the surface water and eventually down through the twilight zone to the seafloor.

"We have three major global-class research ships that are all going to the same study site," says biologist Heidi Sosik. "And each of the ships has a specialized role." Heidi is the lead scientist for the Ocean Twilight Zone Project at Woods Hole Oceanographic Institution (WHOI). WHOI is based on Cape Cod, Massachusetts, and is the world's leading independent nonprofit organization dedicated to ocean research, exploration, and education. Heidi and marine geochemist Ken Buesseler are co-chief scientists on board the R/V *Sarmiento de Gamboa*.

Some fifty different instruments, underwater robots, gliders, and nets will be in the water during this expedition. In addition to all the people on the ships, another team back on land helps coordinate the project.

Covid—19 Precautions

The expedition takes place during the global Covid-19 pandemic. Initially I am concerned about traveling during the pandemic, but I feel more comfortable once I learn about all the precautions in place. Everyone works together to make the expedition happen safely. We test before leaving our home countries, we wear face masks, and we quarantine in a hotel for two weeks before boarding the ship. During that time, each person undergoes two PCR tests: one six days after entering quarantine and the other ten days after entering quarantine. The ship's crew is just as cautious. We remain masked on board the ship for the first five days. In the end, nobody on our expedition contracts the virus.

"One of the most exciting things about this expedition is that we're using a wide range of technologies and different approaches to observe the ocean," says Heidi. "Everything from satellites that are orbiting Earth and can look at big swaths of the ocean, all the way down to cameras that are in the ocean looking at the microscopic scale of the organisms and how they're distributed at different depths."

Pulling off a mission this complex takes years of preparation. Ken headed up the planning for WHOI. He worked alongside scientists and engineers from WHOI, NASA (the National Aeronautics and Space Administration), and several other institutions in the United States and Europe to coordinate all three ships and the land-based crew.

Successfully navigating Covid-19 precautions makes us even more excited to finally be on board the R/V *Sarmiento de Gamboa*, this 71-meter (233-foot) ship that will be our home, laboratory, and transportation for more than three weeks. Everyone has made sacrifices to be here.

Heidi explains, "We can't fail now that we're all here together. . . . We tried to have the expedition last year, and it wasn't possible [due to Covid-19], but we didn't give up. We stuck with it. We planned. We worked really hard to be here."

Ken says, "I'll be very excited to see Vigo [Spain] behind us, leaving these docks, starting this grand experiment with three ships in the North Atlantic. It's going to be wonderful."

Everyone aboard the ship knows three of the biggest reasons the ocean twilight zone is important:

1) The twilight zone has fishing potential. Humans around the world rely on fish protein for food and to feed aquaculture species. According to biologist Joel Llopiz, "To fish the ocean twilight zone sustainably, we need to understand the ecosystem and the organisms that live there." This includes understanding things like how

R/V Sarmiento de Gamboa *tied up at the dock in Vigo, Spain.*

many animals are in the twilight zone, how long the animals live, and when they reproduce.

2) The twilight zone moves carbon from the surface waters to the deep ocean. "The ocean does all kinds of amazing services for the planet and humanity that we sometimes don't appreciate," says Heidi. "One example is that something like half of the carbon that humans have released into the atmosphere has ended up in the ocean. The ocean has provided this great service of keeping the pace of climate change much slower than it would be without the role of the ocean." Scientists know that the twilight zone plays an important role in regulating Earth's climate, but they're just beginning to unravel exactly how that works. And they don't know how it might change as the climate warms further.

3) The twilight zone is populated by supremely weird organisms. Or rather, what seems weird to humans is quite common there. Picture fish with appendages that sprout from their head like a fishing pole and light up to lure prey. Imagine long strings of gelatinous bubbles—colonies of animals called siphonophores—that perform arabesque-like moves and twinkle like stars. And then there's the most abundant vertebrate on the planet: the tiny and fierce-looking bristlemouth. Most are less than 5 centimeters (2 inches) long. In addition, many large animals that people know and care about, such as whales, tuna, and seals, depend on the twilight zone for food.

There's foul weather in the forecast, but after all the hurdles we overcame to get here, Ken believes that the team can handle it. "We'll be dealing with equipment, trying to work safely on a ship that's rocking all the time. We might be taking waves and have to shut down, but we've done that before. That's something we can handle."

In the main lab, long empty benches await equipment that will soon fill the room. An informal meeting breaks out as scientists divvy up the work areas. The tone is collaborative and flexible with an undercurrent of excitement. Everyone is eager to get to work. So am I. I'm on board to write this book, to help document the scientists' work for WHOI's web page "Dive and Discover," and to assist as needed.

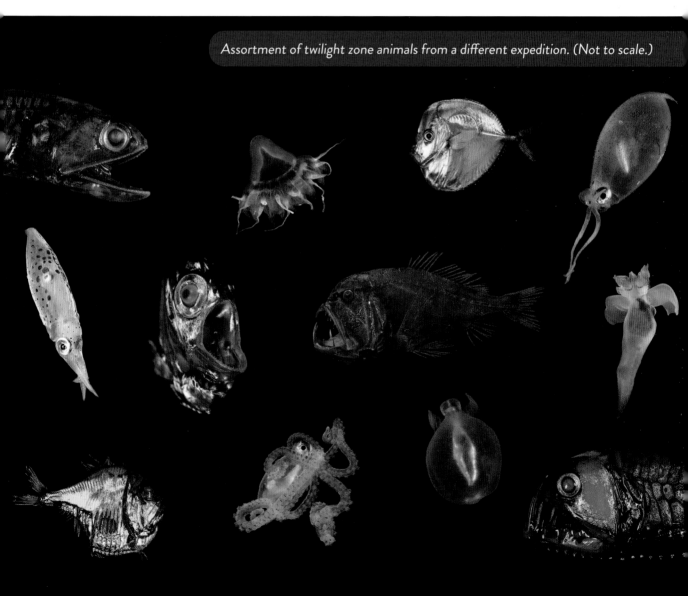

Assortment of twilight zone animals from a different expedition. (Not to scale.)

ALL—HANDS MEETING
April 30 (Day 2)
VIGO, SPAIN • latitude 42.2° N, longitude 8.7° W

All nineteen members of the science team gather in the lab right after lunch. We fill up the available space—sitting on the floor or stools and leaning against counters. The shared anticipation is palpable. Ken gives his perspective on the cruise. "I've been sailing for over thirty-five years, and I've never been a part of an expedition like this one. This is an extraordinary opportunity."

Ken begins reviewing the plans for the day, and then someone calls out, "It's here! I see our shipping container!" The room erupts with cheers and claps. The science equipment was already delayed once. Mobilization—preparing the ship for departure—was supposed to start yesterday. Everyone worried the container wouldn't arrive today, creating another delay.

As Ken hurries out to "break the seal" on the container, Heidi takes over the meeting. She shares three important points that should guide the work on this cruise. She counts them off on her fingers.

1) Safety first. This is a dangerous work environment. We must always wear a hard hat, steel-toed boots, and a PFD on deck. We must always be aware of our surroundings and hold handrails when moving around the ship.

2) Incredible science. The team is here to do cutting-edge science. Everyone must work together to accomplish the expedition goals. People must help others when needed, even if it's not "their job."

3) Amazing personal experience. Heidi reminds us that we want a positive work culture that's collaborative and free from harassment of any sort. She tells us we should speak to her, Joel, or Ken if we

have any problems. She also posts brochures around the lab with directions for contacting people back on land at WHOI if we need outside support.

We gather on the fantail, the back deck of the ship, ready to receive pallets of equipment. This is the first phase of mobilization. (The whole process takes about four days, so even though we already live on the ship, we won't leave Vigo until May 3.) The ship's crew cranes the equipment from the shipping container onto the deck. Then we surround the pallets and hustle to move bins and boxes off the deck and into the lab.

The crane loads equipment onto the ship.

"For months we've had meetings for what the plan would be," says Laetitia Drago, a PhD student from France. "To see someone's eyes light up as their gear comes off the container . . . that is really exciting."

In two and a half hours, the crew and science team move eight tons of equipment. The most impressive item is a 3,000-kilogram (7,000-pound) winch! It looks like a giant spool of thread with a thick cable wrapped around it. It's used to raise and lower heavy equipment into and out of the ocean. Our research vessel has its own winch, but Heidi needs this specialized one to operate the Stingray sled, an important piece of research equipment.

Marley turns to me and says, "I've never seen a science team bring a winch!"

After we've unloaded the container, the pace slows as individual teams begin organizing their workstations. The main lab, which once felt large, now feels cramped. Assorted crates, bins, and equipment fill nearly every open space.

From day one everyone works well together, in part because we got to know one another a bit during our two-week Covid quarantine in Vigo. The nineteen of us stayed in separate hotel rooms, but we

The once spacious lab feels full with all the equipment inside.

exchanged hundreds of messages and met over video, too. We worked out expedition details and arranged for contactless supply sharing. We swapped information about grocery deliveries, Spanish customs, and which restaurants had the best takeout. We also commiserated about the constant jackhammering and stonecutting noises outside. The best part was alerting one another about fun things we observed from our windows. "Dolphins at the mouth of the harbor right now!" "A guy doing laps on the helipad of that ship!" Being in quarantine for so long was challenging, but our chats enabled the group to bond before we went to sea.

"You have to be flexible," explains WHOI Senior Research Assistant Justin Ossolinski. "This is a great group. I knew it would be, based on our interactions during quarantine."

Over the next three days, the ship's crew and the science team prepare for our scheduled departure. Most teams stay up late into the night setting up labs, assembling equipment, and stowing empty pallets, bins, and boxes in the storage area below deck.

Pinchos

Ken sends a group message on our first Sunday on the ship: "Today we get a special Spanish treat. At 2:30 we start our midday meal with pinchos." These are small snacks often served on bread or eaten with a toothpick.

We arrive in the mess and find the tables spread with options such as slices of bread topped with smoked salmon, chunks of cheese, and slices of jamón (Spanish cured ham). The Spanish tortilla—a frittata with potato and onion—is an all-around favorite. We savor the delicate flavor of the eggs alongside bold blue cheese and salty olives. And good news: we'll have pinchos each Sunday on board.

After about thirty minutes, the food is cleared. The science team starts to leave, but then two huge pans of paella are carried out of the galley. Paella is a rice-and-seafood dish common in western Spain. We didn't expect more food, and many of us have already eaten more than enough. We agree that next Sunday we'll eat fewer pinchos so we have room for the main course.

Juan, the head cook, arranges pinchos.

DEPARTURE
May 3 (Day 5), 3:00 PM
VIGO, SPAIN • *latitude 42.2° N, longitude 8.7° W*

The mood is party-like on the fantail. The day we've been waiting for is finally here, and we're on our way out to the North Atlantic Ocean! We gather at the starboard rail and view Vigo from a new angle. We each walked and ran all over this city for our daily hour of sanctioned outdoor exercise during quarantine, but we haven't seen the city from the water. We pass megayachts, container ships, and pristine beaches on our way out.

Cook Assistant Xoan del Pozo Martínez, who is from this northwestern part of Spain, shares details of his Galician culture and points out landmarks, such as the Cies Islands, with the world-famous beach called Praia de Rodas, as we pass them. Marley takes funny photos of people on deck with their long hair flapping in the breeze. They joke that they should start a hair band. We're still masked, so we can't see mouths, but everyone's smile goes all the way up to their eyes.

An azure sky full of puffy white clouds belies the storms we know are brewing out in the North Atlantic.

Excited to leave port!

The A-frame lowers the MOCNESS into the ocean.

CHAPTER 2

DAYS 5–7

OUT TO SEA

ADJUSTING TO LIFE ON A SHIP
May 3–5 (Days 5–7)
THE NORTH ATLANTIC • en route to the study site

THE JOURNEY TO OUR DESTINATION will take about two and a half days, which gives us time to get used to life on board before around-the-clock work begins. Each of us responds differently as we adjust to the ship's constant rocking. Some people feel okay, but others are seasick. Drinking ginger tea or sucking on ginger candy settles some bellies, while others require medicine. Everyone drinks lots of water because staying well hydrated is especially important on a ship. The main rooms tend to be dry, and hydration lessens seasickness. Then there's the ever-present engine noise and the ship's creaking as it rolls with the waves. Even in calm seas, research vessels are noisy. It takes time to settle in and start to feel comfortable. Even still, PhD student John San Soucie says he feels lucky to do something so few people will ever experience.

As I stand on deck, contemplating the vastness of the ocean and how small I am compared to it, I feel the same as John. As far as I can see in all directions, a cloudy gray-white sky blankets an endless steel-gray ocean. Thankfully the seas are calm, and the air is warm for the North Atlantic. I need only a light jacket on deck.

John also feels it's imperative to share the work of ocean scientists with the public. "I think it's important to raise awareness about how cool, interesting, and weird ocean science is. There is still so much we don't know about the ocean—it really is one of the final frontiers."

TESTING, TESTING
May 4 (Day 6), 12:15 PM
THE NORTH ATLANTIC • latitude 44.6° N, longitude 11.6° W

We've been at sea for close to twenty hours when we stop for a test station. Ken worked with the ship's captain to choose an appropriate location to test the scientific equipment and make sure it's all working properly before we reach the study site. This way, if something needs to be fixed or adjusted, everyone has thirty-six hours or so to make repairs on board before we reach our destination.

The tests also provide a chance for the crew to practice safely getting equipment into and out of the water. The science team has never been on this vessel before, and the ship's crew has never deployed some of the specialized equipment. Now is the time to work out any kinks.

STINGRAY SLED
12:15 PM

The Stingray sled is a new piece of equipment for the ship's crew, so they spend a few minutes determining the best way to deploy it. The Stingray resembles a sled that could be used on a snowy hillside, but instead it's towed in the water behind the ship. The sled is equipped with delicate equipment, including a camera that takes spectacular images of twilight-zone animals. The crew uses taglines off both sides of the sled to control how much it moves as the A-frame lifts it and lowers it into the water. The A-frame is located on the stern--the back of the ship. It is used to hoist most of the heavy scientific equipment into and out of the water.

Heidi uses the winch to control how far the sled goes by letting out or bringing in the cable. The winch is now bolted to a metal plate that's welded onto the deck. Heidi and John make sure the sled communicates with the ship via its fiber-optic cable, and then they wind in the cable so the crew can bring the Stingray back on board and secure it.

The Stingray sled reaches the water.

MOCNESS

1:20 PM

The MOCNESS (Multiple Opening/Closing Net and Environmental Sensing System) is a heavy square metal frame with five big nets that taper to the end like a butterfly net. The opening to the nets is 10 square meters (108 square feet)! Getting the MOCNESS safely off the deck and into the water, and getting it back out of the water and onto the deck, are no small tasks. The crew takes time to plan the deployment carefully. Finally, the beast is lifted by the A-frame and slides into the ocean.

"It's our first time working on this ship with this crew. It's nice to start to get in a rhythm before we get to the first sampling site," MOCNESS team member and PhD student Kayla Gardner explains. "When we test the MOCNESS, we do everything we'd normally do on a deployment, except the net will only go to 50 meters instead of a 1,000 meters."

Joel and a technician monitor the MOCNESS while it's deployed.

Once the MOCNESS is in the water, scientists and technicians make sure that they can communicate with it and that the nets release when triggered electronically from the lab.

"We've already tested the MOCNESS's ability to communicate with the lab while it was on deck," says Kayla. "But making sure it still works in the water is important."

Once the MOCNESS is recovered (brought back on board), the scientists on the MOCNESS team practice processing and preserving the organisms caught by each net. This helps the team members get into a rhythm by the time we reach the study site.

CTD ROSETTE
4:00 PM

Next up: the CTD rosette. Even though this piece of equipment includes more than sensors that measure <u>c</u>onductivity, <u>t</u>emperature, and <u>d</u>epth, scientists often use shorthand and refer to the whole instrument as the CTD. It's a staple of ocean science that collects data via sensors and an

---

RESEARCH VESSEL TERMS

bridge: The command center of the ship. The captain and officers run the ship from there.

bow: The front of a ship.

deploy: To release a piece of equipment over the side and into the water.

fantail (or aft deck): The deck at the stern (back) of a ship. Most equipment is deployed from there.

galley: The kitchen of a ship.

line: A rope.

mess: The dining room on a ship.

port: The left side of a ship when facing the bow. (There's a trick to remembering the names for the sides of a ship: the word port has four letters, the same as the word left.)

recover: To bring a piece of equipment back on board from the water.

starboard: The right side of a ship when facing the bow.

stern: The back of a ship.

wire (or cable): A material used to lift, deploy, tow, and recover equipment. Also can include fiber-optic and/or regular cables that allow scientists to communicate with the equipment while it's in the water.

imaging system that photographs particles in the water. It also collects water samples in twenty-four containers called Niskin bottles, which are arranged in a circle around the sensors. Each bottle holds 12 liters (about 3 gallons) of water. The crew and most of the scientists have used the CTD many times, but this is the first time WHOI Research Assistant Erin Frates has worked with one.

"A CTD rosette is such a staple of oceanography, but I had never seen one in action until now," Erin says. "When the hangar doors opened for the test, I was a little giddy inside."

Erin expresses something everyone is feeling: the excitement of getting to work. Once the CTD is lowered into the water on a cable, scientists trigger the individual bottles to close at specific depths. When the CTD is brought back on board, Erin attaches tubing to the bottles and makes sure the water flows out of the bottles properly.

Erin continues, "We had attached the tubing to the Niskin bottles and knew everything fit, so we were making sure that when the bottles were full of water and we turned on the pumps, everything flowed as planned."

At the test station, the scientists also complete some smaller tests, such as using a hand-towed net. Laetitia holds the net over the side to capture plankton near the surface. The team also gets something called the tow fish working off the starboard side. This instrument continuously pumps water into the lab so scientists can use it for a variety of experiments.

OLD MEETS NEW

This expedition weaves together a variety of technologies that span fifty years of ocean science. A WHOI scientist named Peter Wiebe invented the MOCNESS back in the 1970s. It's a tried-and-true technology that works side by side on our expedition with cutting-edge technologies such as the shadowgraph imager, TZEX, and MINIONs. WHOI regularly uses new technologies alongside established ones because each technology provides different kinds of data.

SUCCESSFUL TEST STATION

Everything didn't go perfectly, but this was a successful test station. The science teams learned how to operate with the crew and the vessel, while the crew worked out kinks for deploying the Stingray and the MOCNESS.

One issue did appear: while prepping the MOCNESS for its deployment, the team found holes in some of the nets.

"When we laid out the gigantic MOCNESS nets on the deck," says WHOI Research Assistant Julia Cox, "we found that some of the nets had been chewed by mice while in storage and others had ripped along the seams. Luckily we had a sewing kit. I was happy to sew up the nets. I feel proud that I was helping the team achieve our goals."

Erin connects tubes to the CTD and tests that everything works.

Everyone feels ready, so we head off for the final leg of our journey to the study site, called the Porcupine Abyssal Plain (PAP). The hilly seafloor thousands of meters below the surface inspired the name Porcupine. Three ships, R/V *Sarmiento de Gamboa*, RRS (royal research ship) *Discovery*, and RRS *James Cook*, will meet at PAP in the open ocean in the North Atlantic.

Why did the scientists choose PAP as the location for this experiment? That's a big question with lots of answers.

"We're looking for poop and dead bodies," says Ken. This ends up being a favorite quotation of the expedition. It's an oversimplification of a complex process, but it captures a fundamental reason we're out

Technicians prepare to deploy the CTD rosette with its twenty-four Niskin bottles, which will close at specific depths.

Hatchetfish have a thin body that cuts through the water with barely a trace.

here: to better understand the movement of carbon from the atmosphere and through the ocean. Carbon dioxide is one of the gases that cause climate change on Earth.

"The climate's changing, and the ocean is our biggest sink of human-produced carbon dioxide from the atmosphere," says Joel. "Without it we would be many degrees warmer than we are right now."

Like plants on land, tiny plantlike phytoplankton that live near the ocean's surface take up carbon dioxide from the atmosphere during photosynthesis. When they die, they sink toward the seafloor, carrying the carbon. But if the phytoplankton are eaten by zooplankton (animal plankton), the zooplankton take in that carbon and make it part of their bodies. Zooplankton and other animals release carbon when they respire (breath out), make fecal pellets (poop), or die. The carbon sinks toward the seafloor in dead plankton, fecal pellets, and aggregates (clumps of dead plankton bodies and poop). If a fish or

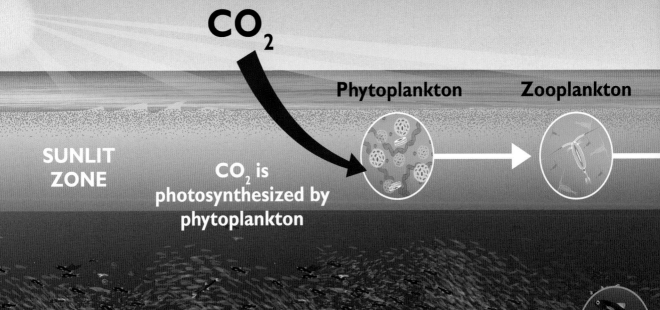

CO₂

Phytoplankton

Zooplankton

SUNLIT ZONE

CO₂ is photosynthesized by phytoplankton

TWILIGHT ZONE

Twilight Zone Creatures

This diagram shows how the biological carbon pump happens in the ocean.

**Apex
Predators**

**Vertical
Migration**

Salp

Carbon below the twilight zone
is trapped for 100+ years

Marine Snow

Salps create
dense, fast-
sinking poop

other animal eats the plankton and swims from the surface down to the twilight zone, the carbon moves deeper. This movement of carbon from the surface to the seafloor is called the biological carbon pump. It includes both the sinking debris and carbon that's moved actively by animals. More carbon is moved to the deep ocean via the sinking particles than by any other pathway.

Scientists strive to understand how much carbon is currently transported to the deep ocean and how it gets there. They also don't know if the biological carbon pump will become more or less efficient as the climate on Earth continues to change.

This part of the North Atlantic has a yearly spring bloom, which means that there is an explosion of phytoplankton growth. Scientists want to understand what happens as that bloom expands and then as the phytoplankton begin to die off. This will help them make better estimates regarding how much carbon gets released back into the atmosphere versus the carbon that's moved to the deep ocean.

Ken says, "We're trying to connect the ocean to the atmosphere to the climate so we can do a better job predicting how those linkages will change as we continue to emit or alter our greenhouse gas emissions, in particular carbon dioxide."

Unraveling these processes is key to understanding the twilight zone's impact on global climate change.

The scientists chose an eddy roughly 100 kilometers (about 62 miles) across as the focus of the research. An eddy is an area where the water moves through the ocean in a circular motion—kind of like a large, very slow hurricane—so anything floating around in there tends to stay together. That makes deploying and retrieving free-floating equipment easier, because it tends to stay at the center of the eddy rather than drifting away. Our ship will continuously crisscross the moving eddy as the scientists conduct their research.

MASKS OFF!
May 5 (Day 7), 9:40 AM
THE NORTH ATLANTIC • en route to the study site

The morning brings exciting news! Ken posts a sign in the lab and sends a group message that we're allowed to take our masks off. We've followed so many Covid precautions that everyone feels confident we can safely stop using masks. This takes getting used to. Most of us have not been unmasked around anyone except the people we live with for more than a year. I find myself grabbing my mask out of habit, even though I no longer need it.

L–R: Julia, Cristina, and Helena prepare for a MOCNESS recovery.

Joel carries a tub of organisms to the wet lab.

CHAPTER 3

DAY 8

THE LARGEST ANIMAL MIGRATION ON EARTH

MOCNESS DEPLOYMENT

May 6 (Day 8), 12:07 PM

THE PORCUPINE ABYSSAL PLAIN (PAP) • latitude 48.9° N, longitude 14.8° W

JOEL PULLS ON HIS STEEL-TOED RUBBER BOOTS, puts on a hard hat, clips into a PFD, and meets the other four members of the MOCNESS team on the deck. The weather is nice today, so he doesn't need foul-weather gear. After traveling for two and a half days, we reached PAP this morning. Over-the-side operations, called "ops," are now in full swing.

Today will be the first deployment of the MOCNESS in the designated study area. The original MOCNESS was designed to solve a problem with traditional fishing nets. When those are towed behind a ship, they catch everything from the surface to the depths and catch more on the way back up, so scientists have no idea how deep each animal was when it was captured. On the MOCNESS, five separate nets are pulled on one tow wire and open and close when directed from the ship. This allows scientists to know at what depth each animal is caught. Scientists around the world now use this system. The long black nets taper down to the cod ends, which are containers that collect the organisms. PhD student Cristina García Fernández and graduate student Helena McMonagle put the cod ends on the nets and wrap them in electrical tape to make sure they won't pop off while in the water. Then Joel and Helena work on one side of the frame while Kayla and Julia work on the other side to "cock the nets." They clip the net bars in place, which enables the electronic triggering to work.

Next the crew takes over for deployment. The ship's bosun—the person in charge of all deck operations—uses a remote control to lift the MOCNESS with the A-frame and slide it into the ocean.

Once the MOCNESS is in the water, technicians on the ship control its movement down and back up. When each net drops closed, it simultaneously opens the net above. During most of the MOCNESS tows on this expedition, one big sample is taken with a single net that remains open from the surface down to 1,000 meters (about a half mile). On the way back up, the rest of the nets are used to sample four specific depths.

Sensors on the MOCNESS also collect data about water conditions and transmit the information back to the ship in real time through the tow wire. The data include things like salinity (how salty the water is), temperature, depth, oxygen, light levels, and how much chlorophyll is in the water (which indicates the amount of phytoplankton).

The data are later matched to the samples collected at specific depths, which helps scientists understand the conditions where the animals live. Knowing where an animal was caught is important to understanding how it migrates and, therefore, its role in carbon movement in the ocean.

Joel heads up the MOCNESS team. According to him, "By knowing what depths the critters came from, and seeing who migrates up and down on a daily basis and who doesn't, we can study the active movement of carbon due to swimming."

Every day during "diel vertical migration," a wave of zooplankton and small fish rise up from the depths to feed in the food-rich surface waters during the night, and then return to the twilight zone during the day. The sunlit (or euphotic) zone is rich with food because enough sunlight passes through the water for photosynthesis to happen. Many of the creatures that spend much of their lives deep in the twilight (mesopelagic) zone move up into the sunlit zone under the cover of darkness to feed on plankton that grew there during the day. When the sun comes up, the twilight-zone animals move back down deep so they can hide from visual predators. This daily migration moves like a wave around the globe as Earth rotates on its axis.

Helena and Cristina haul in the nets on a night operation.

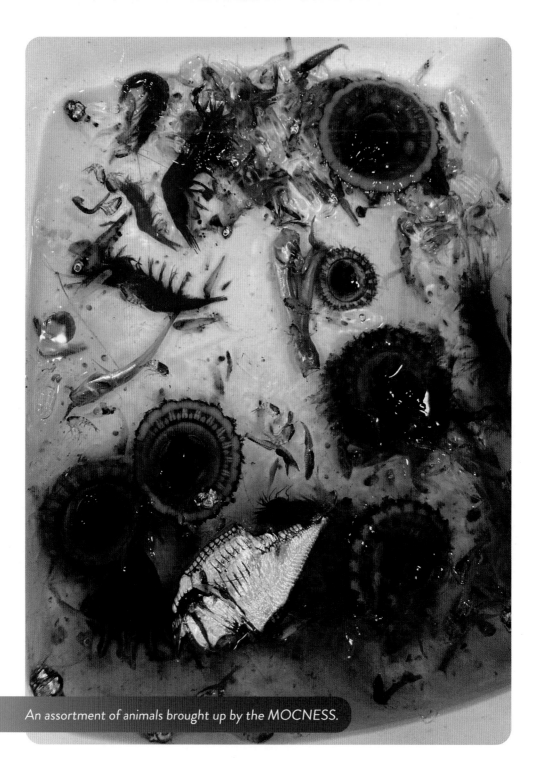

An assortment of animals brought up by the MOCNESS.

"The amazing thing about this is that they're migrating really large distances every single day," says Heidi. "Every night they come up, every day they go down; so we talk about it as the largest animal migration on Earth. And it happens every single day around the planet."

Scientists can use all the data collected by the MOCNESS sensors, combined with the animals they bring up in the nets and the knowledge of how far the nets traveled through the water, to estimate how many animals live in the twilight zone. These data also help scientists determine an animal's preferred conditions. Scientists need to fully understand diel vertical migration in order to clarify its impact on the biological carbon pump.

"We think the animals respond to light levels," says Joel, who studies the fish that make the twice-daily trek. "The critters don't want to be seen because predators will eat them. They go up at night to eat but don't want to be eaten."

Joel continues, "Our night tows are the most important ones because they show us who migrates. The day tows complement them because we can see how far down the animals go."

SEEING RED . . . UNDERWATER

Visible light is made up of all the colors of the rainbow, each with a different wavelength. Our eyes see wavelengths as different colors. In the ocean, longer wavelengths are absorbed faster, so even at shallow depths those colors can no longer be seen. Imagine you're underwater with a plastic rainbow in your hand, and you can go as deep as you want. Red has a long wavelength, so the red disappears shortly after you start to descend, and that part of the rainbow begins to look greenish-brown. Orange disappears next, then yellow, then green, and all colors look black the deeper you go. Blue has a short wavelength, so it penetrates deeply, and that's why the ocean looks blue. Since red never reaches the deep ocean, the red animals there appear black, which makes it hard or impossible for their predators or prey to see them. Many deep-ocean animals are red or black because it helps them survive.

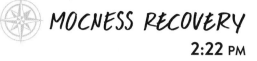

MOCNESS RECOVERY
2:22 PM

As word spreads that the MOCNESS is about to be recovered, members of the science team and the ship's crew gather to watch. While the bosun uses the remote control to wind in the cable, other crew members stand by ready to assist. The A-frame slowly lifts the MOCNESS out of the water and over the deck. As it's lowered, members of the crew place blocks under the frame and strap it down. The whole process is like a well-choreographed dance that gets the MOCNESS back on board as quickly and safely as possible so no one is injured and nothing is damaged.

Kayla and Helena move to the edge of the fantail and clip themselves to a safety strap attached to the ship so they won't fall overboard. Joel, Julia, Cristina, and members of the ship's crew gather behind Kayla and Helena to haul in the nets. As soon as a cod end is pulled onto deck, one person holds the net up while another person hoses it down with salt water to wash any lingering organisms down to the cod end. The nets are so fine that they can catch microscopic plankton along with larger animals such as fish, squid, and sea jellies. The team works quickly to unclip the cod ends from the nets to see if any fish are still alive. Helena scoops any live fish into specimen jars and hurries to a darkened lab on the lower deck to conduct experiments. Helena succinctly explains the question she's investigating: "How do fish move carbon?" She places them in tiny oxygen chambers that measure their respiration rates (breathing).

As Joel says, "The deeper the fish go, the deeper the carbon gets." All living things are made of carbon. As fish move deeper, the carbon in their body goes deeper into the ocean, where it could be released into the water through breathing, pooping, or dying.

Other scientists have collected data related to this, but there's not much information yet because getting live twilight-zone fish to the surface is difficult. The fish live deep in the ocean and go through big pressure and temperature changes during the rough journey in the nets. Helena hopes these experiments will help clarify how much carbon is carried to the deep ocean by fish and released through breathing.

Kayla, Joel, Cristina, and Julia each grab a cod end and carry it to the wet lab, a space specifically designed for working with water. Any spills run back to the ocean through drains in the floor. Kayla empties the cod ends into tubs labeled with the number of each net. Members of the crew and the science team gather to see what was brought up from the deep.

Kayla plunges her hands into the cold water and pulls out one animal after another. Her years of experience tell her this is safe to do. Joel later explains, "Nothing is large enough to bite . . . or pinch. The chance of getting a minor sting is outweighed by the chance of seeing something cool right away—potentially still alive."

A crew member exclaims, "¡Qué chulos los animales!" (What cool animals!)

Kayla has been on many cruises and has processed dozens of MOCNESS tows,

Kayla holds a net, and Julia hoses it with ocean water.

but she says the experience never gets old. "Pulling a net up from the twilight zone is fascinating. It's so diverse and colorful. It's like I'm a kid again. Every net tow is like Christmas Day for me."

Laetitia and I huddle over tubs filled with bright-red shrimp, shiny silver hatchetfish, ruby-red atolla jellies, tiny black lanternfish with their friendly looking round eyes, and lots of transparent animals such as salps and pteropods. My favorite catch this day is a glass squid with delicate red spots and bulging dark eyes. I reach in and gently stroke its smooth, clear body with my pointer finger. Laetitia turns to me with a giant smile and exclaims, "This is what dreams are made of!"

While we marvel at the collection of animals, the MOCNESS team snaps into action. Kayla, Julia, and Cristina process the rest of the samples. Kayla sits on the floor hunched over the labeled tubs and starts with the deepest net first. She gently scoops out any fish she finds and lays them on her left hand. She groups similar fish together, such as hatchetfish and lanternfish. Once she removes all of one kind of fish, she passes them to Julia, who spreads them out on a piece of aluminum foil in a single layer. Meanwhile, Cristina writes a label that lists the tow number, the net number, and the packet number. Cristina also records the data on a master sheet. Julia carefully folds the foil into a neat packet and freezes it in liquid nitrogen. They systematically go through every tub this way.

Once the frozen fish are back in Joel's lab at WHOI, he'll examine the structures in their heads called otoliths, also called ear stones. There are rings on and in the otoliths, and like counting the rings on a tree stump, scientists count them to find out the age of the fish. Once they know how long a type of fish lives and when they reproduce, scientists can better predict the impacts of fishing on that species.

"If we know a fish lives a certain amount of time," says Joel, "and we also know when it starts reproducing, we can assess the population

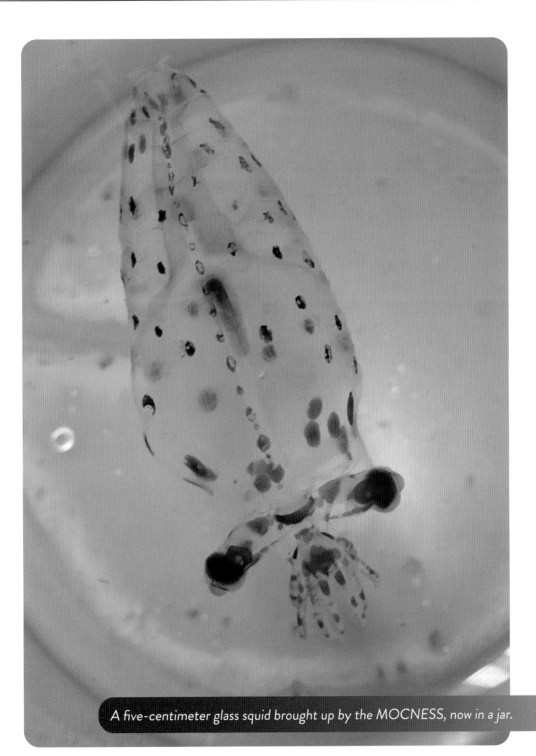

A five-centimeter glass squid brought up by the MOCNESS, now in a jar.

turnover of that species. So if they're long-lived and they don't start reproducing for a long time, then they're going to be less resilient."

In addition, Joel and others will examine the fishes' stomach contents and use a technique called metabarcoding to identify everything the fish ate before they died. This helps scientists understand the complex food webs in this region and how the twilight-zone food web interacts with the sunlit-zone food web when these fish migrate each day to feed.

A collection of lanternfish ready to be wrapped in foil.

"We don't know how much the animals eat at the surface versus how much they eat in the deep," says Kayla. "I'm looking at the bigger picture to see how animals are connected in the twilight-zone food web and how they are connected to surface food webs." In other words, who eats whom? And do they eat more near the surface or in the deep? Kayla does this by analyzing the animals' muscle tissue using a chemistry technique that allows her to determine what a predator ate.

After the initial excitement, tedious work remains. Kayla, Julia, and Cristina remove all the larger organisms until there's only plankton in the

Kayla splits organisms into groups.

tubs. Then they methodically split the plankton in each tub into four equal groups. They freeze some samples and place others in two different preservatives. Each method enables a particular kind of analysis back at WHOI.

They work steadily to get the samples preserved as quickly as possible because they need to stop all biological processes. Even though these tasks take several hours, the women work well together to get the job done.

"Although it's tedious," says Cristina, "it's also entertaining, thanks to the crew and the rest of my colleagues. We make the time go faster by singing silly songs."

As soon as they finish, they return to their cabins to catch a nap before they have to be ready for the next MOCNESS tow. Technically

Bioluminescence

Deep in the twilight zone where little sunlight penetrates, the waters glow with starry bioluminescence. Bioluminescence is light created during a chemical reaction in the cells of certain organisms. Some scientists refer to a kind of plankton called dinoflagellates as a "sprinkling of sea sparkle," due to the way they light up. In some animals, such as lanternfish, light is made in an organ called a photophore. Other animals, such as certain kinds of jellies, create an overall glow.

Two molecules called luciferin and luciferase are needed in order for bioluminescence to occur. Some animals don't have these molecules but instead eat bioluminescent organisms, which enables them to emit light. Others have a symbiotic relationship with bioluminescent bacteria that live in their bodies. Unlike the light from the sun, candles, or light bulbs, bioluminescence is cold.

Why have animals evolved the ability to make light? Some—like the anglerfish—use it to lure prey. Others might use it to attract mates the way a male bird flashing its colorful feathers attracts females. Many animals seem to use bioluminescence as a way to avoid becoming prey. Some squid flash their photophores to scare predators. Certain shrimp eject glowing mucus that confuses predators. A hatchetfish's belly glows, so when predators below look up, the hatchetfish blends in with the dim light coming down from above.

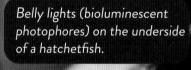

Belly lights (bioluminescent photophores) on the underside of a hatchetfish.

Studying bioluminescence is difficult because many bioluminescent animals are see-through (such as jellyfish) or black (such as bristlemouths). Scientists need bright lights to find them, which scares them away.

two women are on night shift while the other two are on day shift, but today all four of them chose to assist with the MOCNESS recovery.

"The team I have out here works remarkably hard," says Joel. "It's a fairly bare-bones operation, with only two team members on each shift. . . . It's certainly not for the faint of heart to come out here, work so hard, stay up late and get exhausted. . . . Each of the two people who are working with me on each shift is putting in 110 percent. They've been remarkable."

MOCNESS tows are a technology that has been used since the 1970s, but there are limits to what scientists can learn this way. Gelatinous animals get battered by the nets. Fast fish escape. Scientists have no way of knowing what the nets missed. This is where multiple approaches help build a better picture of what really happens under the surface. For example, the Stingray sled provides images of animals that cannot be captured by nets or would be damaged by them. The Stingray is the next big piece of equipment to be deployed.

Bioluminescent atolla jellies emit flashes of blue light.

Deploying the Stingray.

CHAPTER 4

DAYS 8 & 9

CUTTING-EDGE TECHNOLOGY

STINGRAY SLED

May 6 (Day 8), 3:08 PM

THE PORCUPINE ABYSSAL PLAIN (PAP) • latitude 48.9° N, longitude 14.9° W

HEIDI AND JOHN ARE ON DECK for another Stingray deployment. (The Stingray also went out when we first entered the eddy.) John stands ready to operate the winch while Heidi talks to the bosun. The Stingray and the instruments it carries are some of the newest technologies used to understand the ocean.

The crew hooks the sled to the cable and attaches taglines to keep it steady as the bosun rotates the A-frame up and out over the ocean. Once the A-frame is fully over the water, John lets the cable out slowly, using a controller on the winch, until the sled dips below the waves. He continues letting the cable out until the Stingray reaches the desired depth of 1,000 meters (about a half mile). Then scientists control the sled's movements by bringing the wire in or letting it out.

Like the MOCNESS, the Stingray is packed with instruments that measure light, oxygen, and chlorophyll. An acoustic sensor also helps measure the abundance of animals in the twilight zone. The sensor

TIME AND LOCATION STAMPS

All the science that happens on board R/V *Sarmiento de Gamboa* is tracked in an event log. It's a spreadsheet that includes dates, times, and exact locations (in latitude and longitude). There are also columns to record which scientific instrument is used and the action (deployed or recovered). The person logging the data records their name and makes any brief notes that could be helpful later.

Since all of these specific data are important to scientists and their work, I decided to structure the book in a similar way to give a feel for how science happens at sea.

works the same way echolocation does in some animals: the sensor sends sound pulses into the water and listens for the reflection of the sound. Reflected sound indicates that something is in the water. Scientists use the resulting data to estimate how many animals are present.

The instrument on the sled that causes the most excitement is known as the ISIIS (In-situ Ichthyoplankton Imaging System). It can take spectacular images called shadowgraphs, which are pictures of shadows cast by organisms as they flow past the sled.

"Imagine you had see-through skin," says Heidi. "Your bones and muscles would cast a shadow on the wall. That's exactly what happens for many transparent twilight-zone animals. When you shine light on them, their delicate edges and inside parts cast beautiful shadows. We take pictures of those shadows to find these fragile creatures and help identify them and where they live in the ocean."

Heidi, Justin, Marley, and I gather around Heidi's bank of computer screens, eyes wide and staring. Fifteen images per second come into the lab in real time via the cable. Nearly every frame reveals a living thing. The images look like finely detailed charcoal drawings.

Shadowgraphs are particularly useful for capturing images of sea jellies and other jelly-like animals, such as siphonophores and salps, that tend to get damaged by nets. Until recently most of what we know about twilight-zone animals was based on net tows. Detailed shadow-graphs enable scientists to identify which animals live in the twilight zone without having to capture them. The images also help scientists learn more about the gelatinous creatures and make better estimates about how many of them exist.

IMAGING FLOWCYTOBOT (IFCB)

Later Heidi compares what's on her screen to what's on WHOI Research Associate Alexi Shalapyonok's screen.

Alexi sits on the stool at his workstation to Heidi's right. His job is to monitor the IFCB (Imaging FlowCytobot), which takes photographs of plankton found in the water that's continuously pumped to the lab by the tow fish. Alexi's screen is filled with detailed images of diatoms, a kind of phytoplankton.

Heidi and Joel monitor the Stingray sled from the lab.

Heidi and a colleague invented the IFCB to take high-resolution images and measure the details of diatoms and other phytoplankton. The abundance of diatoms suggests the presence of an active bloom— the explosion of phytoplankton that the science team hoped to find in this area of the North Atlantic this time of year.

Heidi messages the group: "This is unlike anything I've ever seen! *Sarmiento de Gamboa* is in an absolute diatom soup!"

This is big news! We're here at the right time. Now the scientists want to study what happens as the plankton start to die.

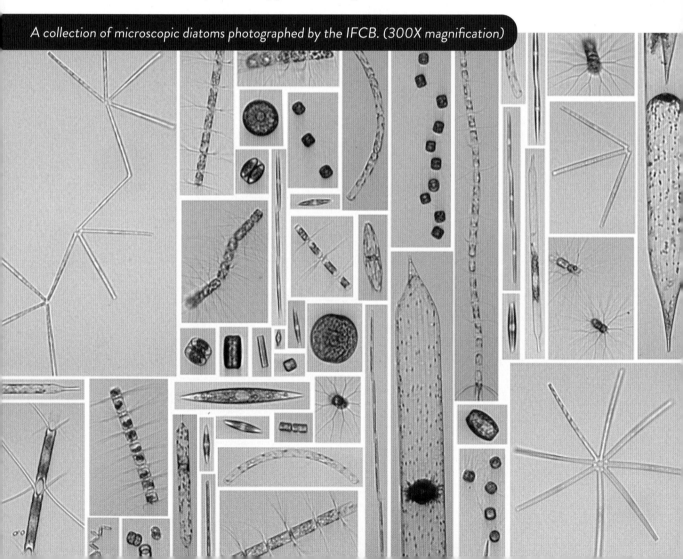

A collection of microscopic diatoms photographed by the IFCB. (300X magnification)

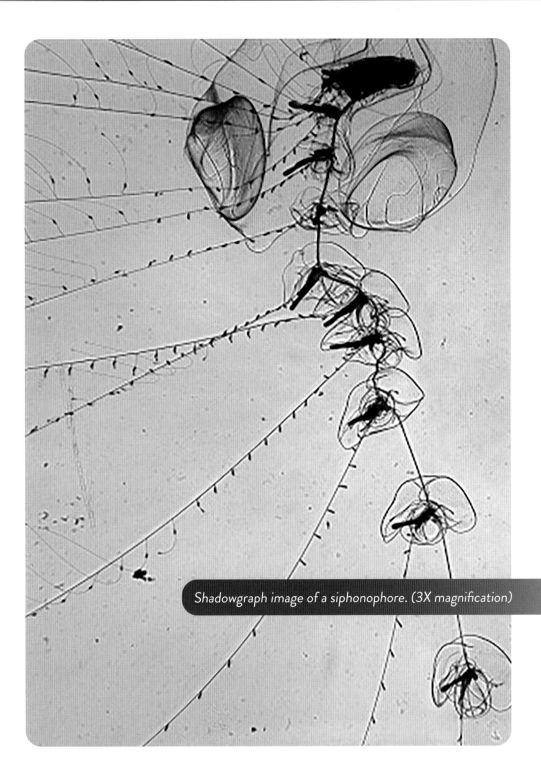

Shadowgraph image of a siphonophore. (3X magnification)

"When the spring bloom is ending and phytoplankton die, we expect to see lots of carbon falling from the sunlit zone toward the deep ocean," Heidi explains. "It's like when tree leaves fall. They land on the ground and decay. When phytoplankton die, they sink, too."

As part of the biological carbon pump, hungry zooplankton (animal plankton) eat phytoplankton. When zooplankton poop or die, the carbon inside sinks deeper. If scientists determine the fate of the carbon, they'll be able to make better calculations about how it regulates Earth's climate.

SO MUCH DATA

Processing the millions of shadowgraph images is a huge task. A scientist or trained technician could look at them and identify individual organisms by sight, but they would spend a lifetime doing that and never finish.

Enter machine learning.

"Now that we have tons of really interesting data about what lives in this region of the ocean that we've never explored," says John, "what tools do we need to actually handle this enormous amount of data and how can we make sense of all of these images?"

John works with artificial-intelligence (AI) software that identifies the organisms in each image in much the same way facial-recognition technology works on a mobile phone. Then humans review how the computer labeled the data to correct mistakes. Over time the technology learns to be more and more accurate.

In order for scientists to draw conclusions from the immense amount of data they collect, they also need a statistical model to describe where plankton live in the ocean and how many are in different places. So John writes computer code that helps process that data.

"We're collecting all this really interesting information about what lives in the twilight zone," says John. "But now we need tools to fully understand what we're looking at. A big part of my job is wrangling the math so that scientists can understand all the data."

A PROBLEM
8:15 PM

John stands on the aft deck, working the winch to retrieve the Stingray sled. His job is to slowly bring it back up from the deep and close to the stern of the ship. Then the crew takes over to lift it onto the deck.

John writes computer code in the main lab.

But something isn't right tonight. As the sled comes up, John notices that the cable is twisted and the armor that protects the cable is crunched. The cable has three jobs: to physically tow the sled (and bear all the weight), to send real-time data back to the ship via fiber-optic wires, and to transmit power to the instruments. The armor protects the important innards of the cable from damage caused by things like seawater and pressure.

John knows the broken armor is a serious problem. Moreover, a

Diversity in Marine Science

There are people on the expedition from the United States, Belarus, Spain, France, Canada, and the United Kingdom. But you might have noticed that most of the scientists and engineers in the photos present as white.

When I met Joel two years before the voyage, he asked if I would include something about diversity in marine science in this book.

He said, "I think it's important for all kids to see themselves reflected in books."

I agree. Joel and I talk about this further in the mess one day. He expands on his ideas and notes that being the first in his family to graduate from college and the son of a Cuban immigrant—even though people often don't know he's Latine—has likely brought perspectives to research teams that enhance not only the science but also the experiences of all those involved. Like so many science fields, marine science has historically been full of white people. Most old photos from WHOI reveal a sea of white faces, nearly all of them men. As recently as the 1970s, Dr. Kathy Sullivan (the only person to both walk in space and visit the deepest point in the ocean—Challenger Deep) was told by one ship's bosun that she wasn't allowed beyond a certain point on the aft deck because she's a woman, even though she had to be there to do her job. (She walked right past him and got to work.)

crew member makes a cutting motion, suggesting that they should cut the cable. John knows that's a dangerous prospect because electricity runs through it. He also knows cutting the cable will end the use of the Stingray on this expedition, and there are still fifteen days left to go.

As soon as the sled is safely back on the deck, John rushes to the lab and yells, "Can someone go get Heidi?"

Heidi is John's graduate adviser and the scientist in charge of the Stingray. She lay down to rest only about an hour earlier after being

Why is diversity in marine science important? "Study after study has shown that when you increase the diversity of perspectives, thoughts, experiences, or feelings in the room, or on a project, you're going to be a more creative team," says Joel. "You're going to have greater impact. You're going to do better work. And that holds for science. If we surround ourselves with white males all the time, we're not going to get those diverse perspectives. The creativity of our science and the impact of our results are going to suffer for it."

Joel is known for mentoring up-and-coming scientists. All the members of his team on this cruise are women. In fact, there are more women than men on the science team on board. Joel and the co-chief scientists hope to recruit an even more diverse pool of marine scientists in the future, especially more people of color.

"I think it's tragic how much we lack diversity in this field," says Joel. "It's a hard nut to crack, for sure, especially as a single individual. But as a PI [principal investigator] who has my own lab, I can make a difference by reaching out and recruiting young scientists from underrepresented groups."

WHOI has also actively worked to diversify for the past several years. Joel serves on WHOI's committee for diversity, equity, and inclusion (DEI). He says, "We've made fairly major strides in the last couple of years, but there is a lot of work left to do."

awake for what seems like days. That's how things go when you're on a ship that runs twenty-four-hour ops: you catch sleep whenever you can. John doesn't want to wake her, but he knows it needs to be done.

John returns to the deck and completes the tasks he was trained to do: he powers off the sled, hoses it down, and puts the caps back on the sensors and shadowgraph lens to protect them while the sled is out of the water.

Then he and Heidi try to determine if they can fix the problem. The solution for the damaged section isn't too bad: they'll simply slide the attachment point up and secure the extra cable on top of the sled so the broken section doesn't need to support any weight.

The twisted cable presents a bigger problem, though. The Stingray can't be deployed with the cable like this—it could break completely,

Heidi and Joel work in the lab.

or data might not transfer correctly. They need a plan. The extraordinary problem-solving skills of marine scientists, engineers, and technicians come into play. They are adept at using whatever tools, materials, and brain power they have on board to get a job done.

John says, "When you impose constraints on people, they get more creative to work around those constraints. That's especially true on a ship."

Heidi and John brainstorm with the marine technicians and members of the crew.

A PLAN
10:45 PM

The proposed solution is unexpected yet somehow not surprising. With help from the bosun, Heidi removes the junction box from the Stingray sled. (That's where connections between the cable and the sled are made.) They use dozens of zip ties—strong plastic connectors—to secure the junction box to a dish rack, a regular old tray used to run dirty dishes through the industrial dishwasher in the mess. They hope the dish rack will protect the sensitive equipment.

Then they lower the dish rack and the junction box, still attached to the twisted cable, into the water off the stern of the ship like any other piece of equipment and wait to see if the cable will untwist.

Think about a swing. Lots of kids lie on their stomach and twist the swing chains or ropes around and around as much as they can and then let go. The swing spins to untwist until it gets back to normal. The same thing happens with a yo-yo. The string might not even look twisted, but when you let it hang, it untwists. Will this work with the Stingray sled cable?

Thirty minutes later the team recovers the dish rack and junction box. It worked! Just like a swing or yo-yo, the cable untwisted as it was pulled behind the ship. They cut off the zip ties and reattach everything to the sled. Then they rinse off the dish rack and return it to the mess. It's back in service cleaning our dishes in no time.

The Stingray junction box attached to the dish rack with zip ties.

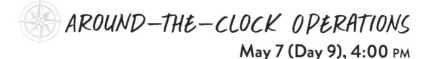

AROUND–THE–CLOCK OPERATIONS
May 7 (Day 9), 4:00 PM

It would be impossible to describe every bit of science that happened between midnight on May 5 and four in the afternoon on May 7, but here's a brief summary.

There were eleven completed deployments and recoveries:

- three CTD rosette casts (one coordinated with the other two ships)
- three Stingray sled tows
- three MOCNESS tows (two coordinated with the smaller MOCNESS on one of the other ships)
- one TZEX test deployment and recovery (more about TZEX later)
- one sound source deployment (helps scientists track instruments in the water)

While all this happened, the tow fish continuously pumped water to the lab for Alexi at the IFCB station, and the ship's underway system provided water for Justin and the mass spectrometer (more to come about this equipment, too). Meanwhile, two other pieces of equipment, one called an Underwater Vision Profiler (UVP) and one called a PlanktoScope, took high-resolution images of plankton.

This much research continues throughout the expedition whenever the weather cooperates. It's a twenty-four-hour operation.

But this pace of work won't last long. A storm is bearing down on us.

The storm out a window.

CHAPTER 5 DAYS 9–12

THE FIRST STORM

THE STORM HITS. Ken's message is forefront in our minds as we finish securing equipment in the lab: "We all want to get to the other side of this storm in good shape!"

We stow our personal items in our cabin and hunker down for what we know will be a long few days. Over-the-side science ops have stopped. It's not even safe for the science team to be out on deck. Deploying equipment is impossible.

The excitement and activity of the past few days is replaced by a quiet, deflated energy. The change hits everyone differently. Marley and I try to work on blog posts for "Dive and Discover," but we're bashed around so much that we can look at our computer screen for only a short time before we feel nauseated. We go to the mess to make ginger tea. Some members of the science team are noticeably missing as they battle seasickness. Even those who don't feel sick struggle with exhaustion. Having your body tossed around is incredibly tiring.

As much as we want to sleep, the storm makes that difficult, if not impossible. I express frustration that my mattress slides in my bunk, and I roll around too much.

Heidi says, "Don't you know the trick? Shove a life jacket or clothes alongside the mattress to stop it from sliding. Roll up blankets and towels to make a nest for your body."

My life jacket, yoga mat, and some clothes fill the space between the mattress and the wall. And when I climb into my bunk again, I wedge folded blankets and towels under my hips. It's not perfect, but at least I roll less than before. I can sleep a little.

I wedged my PFD, yoga mat, and clothes along my mattress to stop it from sliding, and shoved rolled blankets under my body to sleep.

STORM WOES
May 9 (Day 11)
THE NORTH ATLANTIC • various locations

The storm still rages, and it's getting difficult to keep a positive outlook. Storms are always challenging, but we've gone through heroic efforts to get here. No one wants to sit idle for this many days. Ocean scientists always plan for some bad weather days, but facing another day with no over-the-side science ops takes its toll.

Marley and I spend a good chunk of the day lying on the floor of our cabin, staring at the ceiling and sliding back and forth with the roll of the waves. It's a way to rest our muscles, which are tired from working to hold us upright.

Our slides sync up with all the creaks and groans of the ship. *Creeeeaakkkk*. Slide left. *Creeeeaakkkk*. Slide right. Over and over.

Our bodies feel heavy, our brains seem foggy, and we can't concentrate. We move to our bunks for a while. Eventually we make our way to the TV room on the lowest deck and join others to watch old episodes of the show *Friends*.

After dinner the seas have calmed a bit, so most of the science team decides to hang out in the mess. We can't work, so team bonding seems like a good idea. Marley starts off the night by sharing a funny video she made on a previous expedition. Then Helena leads us in a game of *Fishbowl*, a mash-up of word association and charades. We break into two teams, and the challenge is on. There's some friendly trash talk, but people mostly call out encouragement and cheer for successes. The grand finale is Postdoctoral Investigator Elena Ceballos Romero's winning streak. The game ends with her jumping up and down cheering. There's a lot of much-needed laughter.

Then we retire to our bunks to ride out another choppy night.

HITTING A WALL
May 10 (Day 12)
THE NORTH ATLANTIC • *various locations*

At lunch Marley does not seem like herself. Laetitia asks if she's nauseated.

Marley slowly replies, "No, I'm not sick. I just feel like I've hit a wall—mentally, physically, emotionally . . ."

"And literally!" Joel interjects from the end of the table.

We burst out laughing because it's true. We've been slamming into walls for days and have untold numbers of bruises to show for it.

By dinnertime we can't wait to eat, yet we also don't want to. Eating presents a particular challenge on a ship, especially in rough seas. First

A typical dinner in the mess.

everyone needs to walk along the buffet line and serve themselves. Many of us plant our legs wide apart and press our hips into the tray shelf to brace ourselves as we scoop food onto our plate. Then we slide our tray down to the beverages. Most of us don't even try to pour water. Instead, we bring a bottle to the table and pour it there. Getting from the buffet line to a table is particularly hairy because both hands are on the tray.

Someone says, "I wish I had a third or fourth hand available for holding on." That gets a half-hearted laugh from a few of us.

In these conditions the closest seat is the best seat, so the table nearest the buffet fills first. Anyone who arrives late must navigate to more distant tables.

Once seated, people try to relax a little, but that's not usually possible. Things shoot off tables with growing regularity. Pans crash in the galley. As the ship rolls, we lift the sides of our tray—left side, right side, left side, right side—to prevent spillage. On one big roll, our chairs slide sideways. Like dominoes, I slam into Marley, who slams into Justin, who slams into Elena. Elena's chair slides out from under the table, and her glass smashes on the floor. Everyone shifts their chair back into the right place, slides their tray back in front of them, and

MEAL SCHEDULE

Breakfast (two shifts): crew at 7:30, science team at 8:00

Bocadillo, late-morning snack (bread and sliced cheese and meats): from about 10:30 to 12:30

Hot lunch (two shifts): crew at 1:30, science team at 2:00

Merienda, afternoon snack (cookies and tea or coffee): from about 4:30 to 6:30

Dinner (two shifts): crew at 7:30, science team at 8:00

Evening snacks (bread and sliced cheese and meats): from about 9:30 to 11:30

Coffee, tea, yogurt, cookies, bread, and fresh fruit are available anytime.

wipes up the spilled food and drink. Elena stumbles to get the mop and bucket and slams into a pillar. First Cook Juan María Antelo Martínez comes out from the galley to help. Together Elena and Juan clean up the broken glass while skidding back and forth. The whole meal is exhausting.

Despite everything, some science does continue. Justin seems to be in the lab day and night. He stands in front of a tangle of wires and tubes right beside the sink, which feels risky. Justin's highly sensitive equipment—a mass spectrometer—can't get wet. His job is to process

Rough Waters

Marley and I are in our cabin being tossed around by the storm. The ship creaks in a rhythm. Each time the ship rolls slightly farther than the last time, new things bang to the floor. Tonight the bow of the ship slams on the waves, and we hear pans crashing in the galley below us.

The storm has raged for four nights. I've managed okay until now. I haven't felt awesome, but I also haven't really been seasick. But the storm intensifies. The waves are consistently 7 to 8 meters (about 25 feet) high, and we roll close to 30 degrees each way. I'm physically fine, but I'm struggling emotionally.

I sit on the extra bunk with my right foot braced against the ladder to Marley's bunk to keep myself from falling. *Shhhhhhkkkk. Click. Shhhhhhkkkk. Click.* The privacy curtain on Marley's bunk slides side to side.

I'm anxious, but I know there are people on board who can help.

First I message Justin. Even though it's close to midnight, he's still in the lab processing samples. "I hope you don't mind me hitting you up for a little reassurance. This storm has gotten so intense. I'm feeling anxious for the first time and need reassurance that we're okay."

Of course Justin says exactly what I need to hear. He acknowledges my feelings. "Keeping your spirits up for so long when you thought the water that constantly pumps into the lab from an intake below the ship. The trick is to get the water into the mass spectrometer but not on the outside of it.

This is all part of conducting science at sea. Back in the lab at WHOI, keeping Justin's equipment dry is no problem. But now his lab is on a rolling ship. "You can't just take something you do at home and expect it to be exactly the same out here," says Justin.

Justin has draped a couple of plastic bags over the top of the mass spectrometer to protect it from water that might splash up as he works.

yesterday would be the last day . . . it really takes a toll." He tells me the ship is sound and working well. Then he reminds me how amazing the crew and science teams are and says, "You'll get through this; then you'll get through ANYTHING that comes after and have epic stories to tell." He ends by telling me he's available to chat anytime, now or later.

I feel a little less scared. I remember a video call Marley and I had with Elena during quarantine. We talked about the fact that expeditions like this can be a bit scary. Elena said, "There's a lot of wonder we should not miss just because it's scary."

And it's true. Even though I'm uneasy, I still want to be here. There are too many mysteries to uncover.

Marley suggests we get some ginger tea. We make our way downstairs to the mess, getting bashed against the walls. We feel weightless when the ship falls away, followed by a sudden heaviness as the stairs rise to meet our feet.

Sitting with Marley, sipping tea and talking, is exactly what I need. I feel significantly better as we return to our room.

And then we burst out laughing when we reach our doorway and realize that our desk chair has been thrown into the hallway and the trash bin is against the threshold. No matter how well we think we secure things, the power of the ocean seems to break them free.

Even though we're in rough seas, Justin set up his station well, and his equipment keeps chugging along. This machine identifies molecules based on their mass, which tells scientists which chemicals and evidence of living things are in water samples.

"It's working great—surprisingly well, actually," he says. "As long as I have seawater flowing, I'm still able to get bubble-free samples, which allows me to look at the dissolved gases."

Justin's setup is the only one that works continuously throughout all kinds of weather, because water is pumped in from under the ship rather than by equipment that needs to be deployed over the side.

Justin works through all kinds of weather.

Justin's data will help put the rest of the samples collected during this expedition into context.

"It's valuable because we can see what's happening in the storm, and also what happens as the waves dissipate and things return to previous conditions," Justin says. "As we track changes through the storm, we can make some estimates about what the microbes might have been doing."

Meanwhile, when he feels up to it, John works on code to help process data from the shadowgraph imager. Heidi and Joel "teach" the AI software better accuracy by accepting or rejecting labels it applies to shadowgraph images. Marley and I plug away at our posts for "Dive and Discover."

Everyone would much rather be running twenty-four-hour over-the-side science ops, but such is the nature of field science. No matter how well you prepare, sometimes nature has other plans.

Research Assistant Jessica coils a line on deck.

CHAPTER 6

DAYS 13–16

SCIENCE FRENZY

OVER-THE-SIDE OPS RESUME

May 11 (Day 13), 12:35 PM

THE PORCUPINE ABYSSAL PLAIN (PAP) • *latitude 48.9° N, longitude 16.3° W*

TODAY THE SEAS ARE MUCH CALMER than last night. Elena, Kayla, and I are in the mess finishing up bocadillo (morning snack) when Elena notices a message from Ken.

"Oh! The tow fish is back in the water!" she exclaims. "There's going to be a CTD cast soon!"

We go straight to the lab, where preparations are already under way. Just two hours ago not much was happening, but now the change in mood is palpable. Everyone smiles.

Ken has had two mantras during this expedition. One is "This is the plan of the moment." Meaning that this is what we plan to do, but it could change at any time. Sometimes Ken posts the schedule for the day only to change it minutes later as he learns new information about weather or discusses plans with the other two ships.

Ken's other mantra is "The weather will get better." We held on to that idea for three nights. By last night, I wasn't sure I believed him. I should have. Here we are.

Crew members open the hangar like a garage door. They clip themselves in for safety, and the winch lifts the CTD off the floor and pushes it out toward the water. They guide it through the open door, and it's lowered into the water on a cable.

The deepest most equipment on this expedition will go is 1,000 meters (about a half mile), but today the CTD sinks to its deepest point on this cruise: 2,000 meters (about 1.25 miles). There will be a couple of CTD casts to this depth. Scientists want to compare data they collect *below* the twilight zone with data collected *in* the twilight zone. The tops and bottoms of the Niskin bottles on the CTD are open on the way down, so seawater flows freely through them. Once they're triggered to close at designated points on the way back up, water is trapped inside. In the wet lab that water is removed by

Straps keep technicians safe as they deploy the CTD.

different scientists and tested for a variety of properties, such as how much carbon and nutrients are in it.

PhD student Henry Holm organizes the CTD sampling. He determines who needs samples from each depth and then coordinates the order in which each person removes water from the bottles. Henry says, "There's an order to who gets water based on the logistics and the required science."

Henry's research focuses on molecules called lipids in the water. Lipids are a structural part of cells. He seeks answers to the question: What happens to the carbon in those cells as they sink? While Ken's research focuses on how much carbon sinks, Henry asks: What is the carbon made of and how does it change as it sinks?

Henry runs water samples through filters that catch anything bigger than bacteria, and he flash freezes the filters in liquid nitrogen. The filters will be shipped back to WHOI, where Henry and other scientists will use a mass spectrometer to measure the lipids in each one.

Henry processes water samples.

Henry says he enjoys the sensory experience of working directly with the samples as they come back from the deep and notes that "the water from the depths is physically cold." He can always tell which samples came from two thousand meters because the water is near freezing. Working directly with the water out at sea is different from an average day at work on land. "A lot of the work that we do is sitting behind computers after the fact," says Henry. "So it's kind of cool to be here with our samples at the start."

Another approach used during this expedition is environmental DNA (eDNA) analysis. As animals swim through the water, they shed DNA in different ways, including in their poop.

Erin pumps water directly from the Niskin bottles through a filter that collects eDNA. Then she stores the filters in a -80 degree Celsius (-112 degree Fahrenheit) freezer to preserve them. The samples will be sent back to WHOI on dry ice. There, Erin and others will extract the DNA and send it out for barcode sequencing, a process that helps identify specific species of organisms. The DNA caught by the filters will yield thousands of barcodes, which indicate traces of different animals collected in the filters. Scientists will compare the barcodes to a reference database to determine which animals were in the area where the eDNA was collected.

Using eDNA is like doing forensic science in the ocean. If police investigate a crime scene, they might collect fingerprints. Then they

Laetitia prepares to take water samples from Niskin bottles on the CTD.

compare those fingerprints to a database of known people to see if they can find a match. Not every person alive is in the database, but it continues to grow as more prints are collected. Similarly not every eDNA sample will match to a species, but the data are still useful because they help scientists understand the diversity of animals in the twilight zone. This is especially useful for animals—such as fish that avoid the nets—that might be missed in traditional types of sampling.

In addition, scientists will examine eDNA alongside sensor data gathered from the CTD and other technologies used on this cruise to better understand what animals live in the twilight zone and how they move.

Justin continues testing water samples brought up by the CTD, while Alexi and Laetitia take high-resolution photos of plankton. These photos will be used to visually identify the plankton.

We're not back to full operations yet. The seas are still too rough to deploy any other equipment. But after four days, the team is excited to get back to doing what they came here to do.

Salps: Super Poopers

Salps—jelly-like animals abundant in the twilight zone—are fondly referred to as "super poopers" by many scientists. Why? After these animals eat zooplankton, they expel dense fecal pellets (poop!) full of carbon. The pellets sink more quickly than other marine snow particles. If they reach the deep ocean, then there is less carbon in the atmosphere, since it could be trapped on the seafloor for thousands of years. This could have huge implications for global climate change, since carbon in the atmosphere (in the form of carbon dioxide) affects our climate.

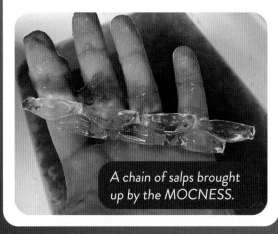
A chain of salps brought up by the MOCNESS.

MINIONS DEPLOYMENT
May 12 (Day 14), 10:10 AM
THE PORCUPINE ABYSSAL PLAIN (PAP) · *latitude 49.1° N, longitude 15.0° W*

Engineer Jackson Sugar stands at a workbench in the lab making final preparations for the first deployment of tiny robots called MINIONs, short for MINiature IsOpycNal floats. *Isopycnal* refers to imaginary lines that indicate ocean water of the same density, and MINIONs sink to layers of the ocean based on density rather than depth.

MINIONs are one of several kinds of technology used on this expedition to measure marine snow: the constant stream of dead plankton and fecal pellets (poop) that rain down from the ocean's surface to the seafloor. As these small robots—each about the size of a two-liter soda bottle—drift in the currents, marine snow lands on a clear glass top, where it is photographed at specific intervals. Meanwhile, sensors record data about the water conditions. Future versions of MINIONs will also have cameras that point out the side and measure how quickly particles fall.

Understanding how much and how quickly marine snow falls is key to understanding the amount of carbon taken from the surface and delivered to the deep ocean. That knowledge helps scientists guide world leaders as they decide how the deep ocean should be used.

MINIONs are still in the development stage. Scientists and engineers constantly dream up new ways to collect data about the ocean, but getting from an initial idea to a fully operational tool takes time. Designing a new piece of technology has four basic steps:

1. Ask scientific questions.
2. Design technology needed to test the questions.
3. Test the technology.
4. Do the science.

MINIONs are currently in step three.

"It's still a prototype—we're working out the kinks," Jackson says.

Compared to most of the other equipment used on this expedition, MINIONs are inexpensive and easy to make. Jackson says, "You could build one in your bedroom!"

MINIONs employ simple electronics that many students use in school, such as Raspberry Pi and Arduino Nano. These electronics provide the most cost-effective way to build the devices because they're inexpensive, readily available, and programmed using Wi-Fi.

Jackson says, "As an engineer, I would never reinvent the wheel." Meaning he wouldn't build new electronics when he can use ones that already exist.

Jackson prepares a MINION for deployment.

The Pyrex (strong glass) tubes that house the equipment on the MINIONs are also inexpensive because they've been repurposed from old scientific instruments. Other parts of the MINIONs are 3D printed using wood filament.

Two MINIONs rest in foam cradles bungeed to Jackson's counter. There's also a set of needle-nose pliers, a spool of fishing line, an assortment of fishing weights, and a tackle box full of individually wrapped Life Savers candies.

What are the Life Savers for? To help the MINIONs sink into the twilight zone. Weights enable the MINIONs to break through the top layer of the ocean. Once they get to the correct depth, the weights must drop off or the MINIONs will keep sinking to the seafloor. That's

Close-up of a MINION on a workbench.

where the Life Savers come in. Weights are attached to one of the candy rings, which is attached to the MINION. When the MINION is lowered overboard and into the ocean, the water dissolves the candy. Once the candy ring breaks, the weights fall off and the MINION reaches neutral buoyancy in the twilight zone, which means it hovers at a desired depth rather than sinking deeper or rising back to the surface. Not all Life Savers are up to this task, however. The ones that dissolve at the correct rate are individually wrapped fruit or butter rum ones, which are larger than those in a roll.

Julia and WHOI Research Assistant Jessica Kozik assist Jackson by tightening up the screws on two MINIONs. Jackson attaches a pre-made bundle of fishing weights to a Life Saver and ties one to each MINION. Then they carefully carry the MINIONs to the aft deck for deployment. After many gray days, we all welcome the patches of blue sky peeking from behind clouds. There are still some whitecaps on the ocean, but today's rolls are gentler.

To make sure the Life Savers break at the right time underwater to release weights, Jackson partially dissolves them—in his mouth!

Jackson works with the bosun to coordinate deployment. MINIONs are sensitive equipment, so they can't simply be tossed overboard. Instead, Jackson wraps a line around a MINION and then pulls part of the length of line through a loop. He slides the metal end of a screwdriver through the loop's opening and then pulls the line tight. A different line is attached to the handle end of the screwdriver. When Jackson lowers the MINION into the water, he tugs on the line that's attached to the screwdriver handle. The screwdriver comes out of the loop, the line around the MINION loosens, and the MINION sinks below the waves. And Jackson still has the screwdriver to repeat the process with the next MINION.

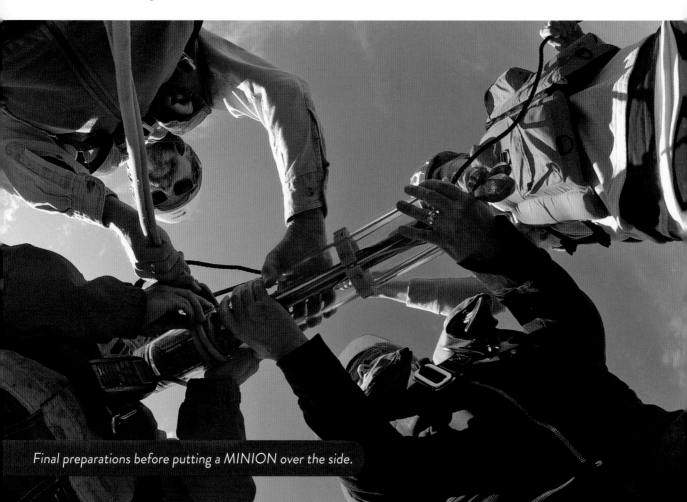

Final preparations before putting a MINION over the side.

Once all four MINIONs are safely deployed, the bosun slaps Jackson on the back and says, "I like your method because it's very simple!"

Simple is the point. In the future, MINIONs will be deployed for a period of days or weeks. During this expedition, however, they're programmed for missions ranging from ten to twenty-four hours to test how well they work.

Excitement and anticipation are in the air as the MINIONs disappear beneath the waves. Will they do what they're supposed to do and return to the surface? If so, will we be able to find them?

"This isn't the first time I've deployed MINIONs," Jackson says. "But this is definitely the most challenging location in terms of sea state. I'm cautiously optimistic."

Deploying a MINION. Tugging on the black line causes the screwdriver to slide out from the loop and the MINION is released.

In order for the MINIONs to float back to the surface, even more weight must drop. Once a mission is complete, an electronic current in each MINION triggers a "burn wire" which releases more weight, and the MINION floats back to the surface. It sends its location data via satellite, and a light on the MINION flashes so scientists can find it at nighttime. (Though that can take a while! The ocean is big, and MINIONs are small.)

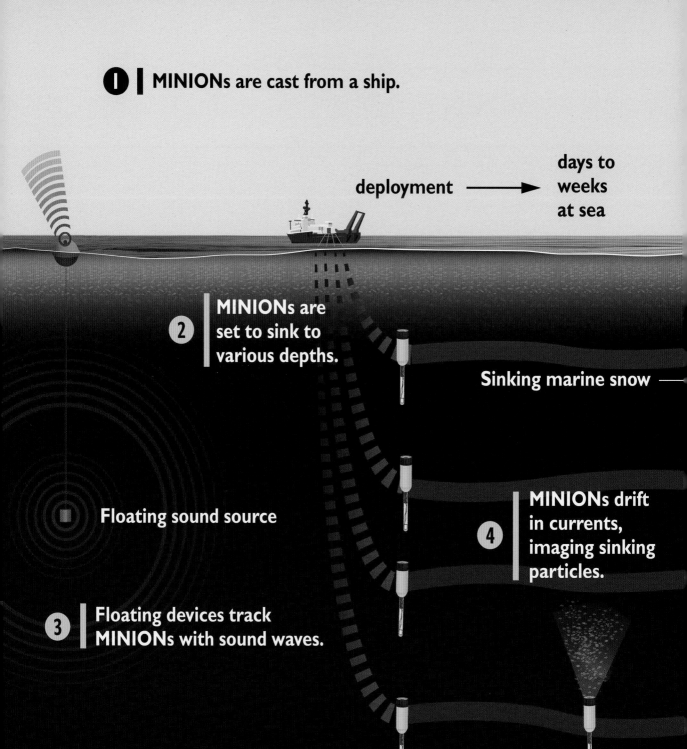

1 | MINIONs are cast from a ship.

deployment ⟶ days to weeks at sea

2 | MINIONs are set to sink to various depths.

Sinking marine snow

4 | MINIONs drift in currents, imaging sinking particles.

Floating sound source

3 | Floating devices track MINIONs with sound waves.

How the MINIONs work.

recovery

camera

stereo-imaging

hydrophone

temperature, pressure & oxygen sensors

After days to weeks, MINIONs drop weights and float to the surface, where they transmit data via satellites.

⑤

burn wire

drop weight

Pressure-resistant glass housing

MINION

MINIONS SEARCH
May 12 (Day 14), 8:20 PM
THE PORCUPINE ABYSSAL PLAIN (PAP) • latitude 49.1° N, longitude 14.8° W

A bunch of us are in the mess chatting after dinner when we receive a message from Ken. "Anyone with binoculars or just good eyes is welcome on the bridge to spot MINIONs."

A MINION pinged its coordinates when it reached the surface, and now we need to find it. Several of us climb the stairs to the dark and quiet bridge and spread out across the bank of windows. The light on the MINION is programmed to flash at random intervals so it doesn't match up with the rising and falling waves. All eyes are on the sea.

"Rebel Rebel" by David Bowie begins to echo through the room. A few heads bob. Some people mouth the words. I sing along quietly while keeping my eyes glued to the water.

After we've been searching for about twenty minutes, Justin spots the flashing light. The rest of us strain our eyes until we each see it off the bow. Locating this small piece of equipment in the middle of the North Atlantic feels like a little miracle. The truth is that careful engineering made it possible.

While the captain navigates toward the MINION, we head down to the aft deck. Jackson and members of the crew mobilize to retrieve the MINION. This will be the first recovery of untethered equipment— not attached to the ship by a line or cable—during this expedition.

We gather at the port rail in the darkness, watching the flashing light until it's close enough to reflect off the hull. The sea is still pretty rough. Someone shines a spotlight on the MINION. Energy levels are high as members of the crew reach over the side with long-handled fishing nets to catch the MINION. They make several attempts but miss.

Someone exclaims, "Oh, no! So close!"

Crew members with nets stumble past me in the darkness, hoping to catch the MINION. We watch it drift alongside and behind us. We feel deflated, but there's no time to wallow. The captain brings the ship around for another pass.

This time a crew member scoops it out of the water before it can get away. Cheers ring out in the darkness. Jackson enters the lab and holds the MINION aloft, triumphant.

Later Jackson will wirelessly download all the data the MINION collected on its tiny computer.

Jackson holds a MINION after a successful recovery.

✴ THREE SHIPS, ONE DRONE
May 13 (Day 15), 11:45 AM
THE PORCUPINE ABYSSAL PLAIN (PAP) • latitude 49.1° N, longitude 14.7° W

The air is warm and sunshine glints off the water. I spread a white bath towel on the deck. Marley places a videography drone in the center of the towel and checks the controls. She's charged with documenting this unprecedented gathering of three research ships in the North Atlantic. The drone's flight could be tricky. Marley's small drone can be flown in winds of up to 15 knots (about 11.5 miles per hour). The wind speed hovers around 10 knots and the gusts are stronger. Plus, the ship still rolls side to side, even though the seas have calmed. Despite the risk, Marley decides to go for it.

She signals to everyone that it's a go. The drone lifts straight up and moves toward the other two ships, RRS *Discovery* and RRS *Cook*. I keep my eyes on the drone while Marley watches the controls. The drone gets pushed around in the wind, but Marley keeps her cool. She flies it high off the port side and over us to

THREE SHIPS ARE BETTER THAN ONE

Why are three ships involved in this expedition?

"That's a unique thing," says Ken. "We actually need three because there are so many different measurements we want to make, and we physically can't fit on one ship. Plus there's not enough time in the day, even though we work twenty-four hours a day, seven days a week when we can. It takes three ships' worth of people and resources to make the biological rate measurements that are needed."

The ships also take some simultaneous measurements so they can compare results. For example, when the ships line up during the drone flight, they do simultaneous CTD casts.

"We wanted to see that we were getting the same readings," said Henry. "That fundamental check between ships was an important part of the expedition."

There were also coordinated MOCNESS tows to make comparisons among what each ship caught.

the starboard side to catch footage of the three ships in a line. Then she takes one more pass before indicating that she's ready to land.

Landing a drone on a rolling ship is difficult enough, but Marley has the added challenge of 10-knot winds, so we decide I should catch it. The towel will provide a soft landing. I stand with my legs wide apart and knees slightly bent with the bath towel draped across my open arms. As Marley slowly guides the drone toward me, a gust of wind pushes it backward and to the left toward the rail. My adrenaline pumps. Marley finally gets it close. It bounces off the towel to the right. I lunge forward and catch it, careful not to damage it. Everyone on deck hoots and cheers. Marley throws her arms in the air while I clutch the drone gently to my chest.

Marley navigates the drone to land on the towel across my arms.

The word *epic* gets thrown around a lot, but it seems to apply here. WHOI has audacious plans for their study of the ocean twilight zone. Of course they'd stage an impressive drone flight to document the project and eventually share it with the world.

The three ships gather for simultaneous sampling.
L–R: RRS Discovery, *RRS* James Cook, *R/V* Sarmiento de Gamboa.

REENERGIZED
May 14 (Day 16)
THE PORCUPINE ABYSSAL PLAIN (PAP) • *various locations*

Everyone has been working for three days straight, running twenty-four-hour ops while the weather is good. Frenetic energy hums among the science team. Many of us run on pure adrenaline.

Elena predicted this. She said, "Keeping pace with all of the high-speed goings-on with science can be challenging. There are so many things going on simultaneously. You try to get yourself involved in as many as you can. It's keeping pace without losing your mind and your sleep."

Elena is exactly right. People grab naps when they can but otherwise work to cram in as much science as possible before the next storm blows in. After days of lying around and killing time, everyone finds the current nonstop work exhilarating.

"We're all so reenergized," says Heidi. "Getting back to work and getting data and samples—it feels amazing."

And then another storm hits, and all over-the-side ops cease again.

Another storm seen from the bridge.

THE SECOND STORM

GALLEY COOKS: UNSUNG HEROES

May 15 (Day 17)

THE NORTH ATLANTIC • various locations

I STAND AT THE OPEN DOOR in the wet lab. Yellow caution tape reminds me not to go out on deck. The rough seas make it unsafe to be out there. The tow fish chugs along outside—sounding like a snare drum with its *ratta-tat-tat*—pumping water into the lab. I focus on the distant gray horizon and breathe the salty air in deeply. My uneasy stomach calms.

I turn and make my way toward the mess in search of a snack. I've learned that I need to keep my belly full to feel my best when the sea is rough. With an empty stomach, I start to feel vaguely nauseated, and I know it will get worse if I don't eat. A little bread and cheese do the trick. I stare out a porthole and watch the dark sea crash and send up sprays of white, and I think about food and interruptions during the voyage.

Keeping forty-three people well-fed is no small task. Add the fact that two cooks prepare three meals plus two snacks each day in a galley that constantly rolls with the waves, and the job becomes even more difficult. Juan and Xoan handle all aspects of the galley on R/V *Sarmiento de Gamboa*, from ordering supplies before departure to preparing and cooking meals to cleaning dishes and pans.

Their day starts each morning at 6:30 when they wake up to prepare breakfast, and it ends sometime after nine at night after they clean up from dinner.

Even in the worst storms when we're all bashed around by the waves, Juan and Xoan must prepare meals. With only two of them available to work in the galley, they can't get sick. They have to be ready every day, all day. Somehow they do it with smiles for more than three weeks. Juan says, "I'm just doing my job," but we know these two men bring a level of cheer that makes eating while holding on for dear life bearable. They know that a well-fed crew is a happy crew. Everyone works hard, so arriving in the mess to find homemade pizza or chicken curry or an almond cake baked for someone's birthday makes any day better.

The mess is noisy. Even on the calmest days, cooking sounds waft out from the galley alongside aromas of our next meal. Sometimes there are clanging pans or whirring stick blenders as Juan beats ninety eggs for omelets. Other days there's the pungent smell of garlic sautéing in oil. And every day Juan's eclectic playlist booms from his

Sample Dinner Menus

We ate delicious and varied foods for three weeks. Vegetarian options were also available.

Rice, chicken curry with vegetables, roasted potatoes, roasted cod, and naan (flatbread)

Roasted rosemary potatoes, fish, green beans, and salad

Three kinds of pizza (veggie, cheese, and cured meats) and salad

Spaghetti with meat sauce, green beans and tomatoes topped with hard-boiled eggs, and salad

Fried eggs, french fries, coleslaw, and bread

travel speaker. One morning during bocadillo, the songs change from "Dancing Queen" by ABBA to "Crawling" by Linkin Park. We laugh at the strange combinations.

Xoan says the cooks don't really have one job. They have many, including dishwasher, cook, therapist, and clown. Indeed, both men do all these jobs well. They keep our bellies full of good food, they notice if someone is having a bad day and check how they can help, and they smile and crack jokes to keep the mood light.

Juan, the head cook.

THINGS WILL GO WRONG

The science team did their best to plan ahead for every contingency, right down to the smallest details, but there is a universally accepted truth about science at sea: things *will* go wrong. How the team responds to challenges that arise affects the success of the mission. Some problems cannot be solved while in the middle of the North Atlantic, but the vast majority can, or at least they can be mitigated.

The first step in problem-solving at sea happened before we left shore: packing extras. The teams packed everything they thought they could possibly need, knowing that they wouldn't be able run to a hardware store to pick up a part. This means extra batteries, tools, bungee cords, and specimen containers. They also packed a variety of tape, including duct tape, packing tape, and electrical tape. And they packed zip ties. Lots and lots of zip ties. Regardless of who packed what supplies, everyone shares once on board. If a scientist forgot a ratchet strap, for example, and someone else has extras, they share without question. Everyone works together for the success of the mission. Problem-solving at sea requires sharing supplies, ideas, and expertise.

As Justin says, "One of my favorite parts of going to sea is that all of my problems are in the length of the ship. This is a 71-meter [233-foot] ship, so that means all of my solutions are also in the same 71 meters of space. When a problem comes up, you find a way to make it work. You often rely on electricians, the deck crew, the captain, the PIs [principal investigators], and the scientists, and you find a way to get it done. I love that aspect of it."

Justin's observation proves correct over and over again on this cruise. When John needs to secure the wires from the Stingray sled overhead so people won't get hooked on them, he asks me to assist. He attaches the wires to the tip of a wooden pole, and I hold the pole up while he zip ties it to the winch frame overhead. The MOCNESS team finds another hole in one of the nets, so Julia sews it up with the

Julia sews a damaged net from the MOCNESS.

needle and thread the team brought. When a metal piece breaks on the MOCNESS, one of the technicians welds it. Over and over again, the team faces the problems that arise—some small, some more significant—and deals with them. Sometimes equipment breaks and can't be repaired, so the team finds a workaround. For example, for a couple of MOCNESS tows, some of the nets weren't used because of the broken part.

One problem the team can't fix is the ongoing bad weather, so we focus our attention on making the best of the situation. Even though over-the-side operations can't happen at the moment, as long as the tow fish keeps chugging along, the IFCB takes high-resolution photos. Alexi makes sure things still run smoothly with the IFCB, and he takes a break to read a book. When living and working in such close quarters, it's important to find pockets of time for yourself.

BATTLING BOREDOM

With so much downtime, people search for ways to keep busy. Some binge-watch shows and movies. Others read or write. When the ship isn't rolling too much, Joel goes for rides on

HEAVING SHIP

The R/V *Sarmiento de Gamboa* pitches and rolls all over the place, even during reasonably calm seas. The experienced scientists aboard confirm that it rolls far more than most research vessels. When we bring the three ships together for a simultaneous CTD cast, someone on one of the other ships messages that we look like a bath toy bobbing around.

Why does this ship roll so much? There are three reasons:

1) Wide beam (the ship is wide relative to its length)

2) Shallow draw (the ship doesn't sit very deep in the water)

3) Light load (we're not carrying lots of provisions or heavy equipment)

This ship makes regular trips to Antarctica to deliver supplies to Spanish researchers, so it usually carries a much heavier load. A ship that sits higher in the water moves easier but also rolls more.

the road bike he brought on the ship, set on a stand, and converted into a stationary bike.

Other activities provide opportunities for group bonding. One favorite pastime is darts. In the early days of the expedition, members of the crew often gather on the lower deck in the bow to play. Eventually members of the science team join them. Everyone stays far away from the dartboard because rogue darts are common when seas are choppy. People laugh together as they avoid flying darts and get to know one another in new ways.

The daily workouts that break out in the TV room are a little more intense, but there's lots of camaraderie as Kayla and Marley lead people through rounds of squats, arm exercises, or leg lifts. They crank up the music and dig deep to do more repetitions. People occasionally topple over when the ship rolls, and that leads to rounds of laughter.

A technician welds a broken piece from the MOCNESS.

One activity that draws in nearly everyone is decorating Styrofoam cups. Once the weather breaks, they'll be secured inside the legs of a pair of pantyhose and zip tied to the outside of the CTD before a cast. Why would we do that? The pressure of the deep ocean shrinks them, creating a fun souvenir of our trip.

Shrunken cups, back from 2,000 meters deep.

THINGS WILL GET BETTER, RIGHT?
Sunday, May 16 (Day 18), 8:00 AM
THE NORTH ATLANTIC • various locations

I look forward to coffee each morning, but I know that in rough weather I can't simply set my cup down. I need to constantly tip my tray up and down with the waves to keep liquid from sloshing out, or hold the cup in my hands and sway with the motion. When big waves come through, we tend to laugh and make jokes, but we're weary. Lack of sleep makes us tired, but the constant battering of our bodies really gets to us.

At breakfast Julia hoists her cereal in the air to prevent it from spilling during a big roll. With both her hands on the bowl, she can't hold on to the table. Her chair skids across the mess. When it stops, the chair is partially under another table with Julia bent over and still holding her bowl. Remarkably none of her cereal has spilled. Julia moves herself back to her original table and continues eating.

We're so ready for this storm to be over. Ken tells us tomorrow is looking better. We hope he's correct.

TZEX going into the water.

UNDERWATER ROBOTS

TZEX DEPLOYMENT
May 17 (Day 19), 5:30 PM

THE PORCUPINE ABYSSAL PLAIN (PAP) • latitude 48.9° N, longitude 14.8° W

AS ALWAYS, KEN IS RIGHT. The storm finally passes, and Jessica, Ken, and Elena gather around the Twilight Zone Explorer (TZEX) on deck. Jessica uses her laptop to do a final check on each system. Since everything runs properly, TZEX is ready for deployment.

We're in the final days of our expedition, and another storm is expected to hit on our last day at the study site. The team commits to cramming in as much science as possible between now and then. TZEX, one of the new technologies being tested in the open ocean for the first time on this trip, is up next. It's programmed to go 300 meters (984 feet) deep to collect samples and data and then return to the surface.

Unlike the MOCNESS or the Stingray sled, TZEX is not connected to the ship. Rather, it drifts with the currents like MINIONs do and floats at a specific depth programmed by scientists before it's deployed.

"TZEX is one thing I'm really excited about," says Ken. "My lab and the engineers at WHOI have been working on it for close to a year now."

TZEX is a sediment trap that records marine snow as it sinks from the sunlit zone down through the twilight zone. Think of it like a rain gauge. Instead of collecting rain that falls from the sky, it collects marine snow as it falls through the water. Ken will analyze the particles in his lab back at WHOI. TZEX also takes high-resolution

Expeditionary Behavior

In his book *An Astronaut's Guide to Life on Earth*, Colonel Chris Hadfield says that "expeditionary behavior" is defined as "the ability to work in a team productively and cheerfully in tough conditions." While ocean scientists don't use Hadfield's phrase, they do refer to "being a good shipmate."

The premise is basically the same: people need to work as a team, especially when outside their comfort zones and in dangerous conditions. Hadfield also says that when things get difficult, team members can choose to "wallow in misery" or they can "focus on what's best for the group." He says, "Searching for a way to lighten the mood is never a waste of time."

Indeed, all that is true on this research expedition. The team isn't in outer space, but living and working on a research vessel in the North Atlantic comes with its own dangers and challenges. Whether it's day three of a grueling twenty-four-hour schedule, or the fourth day in a row of stormy seas, members of the crew and science team repeatedly demonstrate that they are good shipmates. If a peer has a problem with equipment, someone jumps in to help. If a team member has a difficult day, others look for ways to lighten their load. And during times when everyone feels stressed, people often crack jokes. Everyone knows that the success of the expedition lies in our ability to work together and manage our physical and mental health.

photographs that provide evidence of what's around during sampling. Unlike a MINION, which uses weights to sink and drops them to float, TZEX sinks and rises by deflating or inflating an oil bladder.

The team deployed TZEX once before the ship left Vigo to make sure it was weighted correctly, but the relative calm of the harbor is nothing compared to open-ocean deployments. Any number of things could go wrong, causing this expensive piece of equipment to be lost. Priority one: safely deploy and recover the instrument. Later the team will make any needed adjustments to improve data collection and functionality.

Today is the second deployment at sea, since TZEX was out for about twenty-four hours five days ago. There were a few glitches during the first deployment, such as a line wrapping around the top, so today the team focuses on making the deployment smoother and more efficient.

The bosun lowers a cable from the crane and hooks it to the top of TZEX. Then the crane slowly lifts it from its custom-made wooden cradle. Two members of the crew stabilize TZEX with taglines to prevent it from swinging too much as it's moved out over the starboard side and lowered into the water. Everything goes smoothly this time.

The team smiles as they watch it sink below the waves, and they hope to see it successfully returned to the deck tomorrow night.

A SURPRISE
9:30 PM

About four hours later, we get an exciting message from someone on RRS *Cook*. "Why search for the MINIONs when they come to us?"

This is amazing news! A MINION pinged earlier, but it was too far away from our ship, and we were running out of time. Ken had made the difficult decision not to go after it, but it's close to the other ship's location.

The RRS *Cook* team reports their efforts in real-time messages. "We are slowly trying to creep up onto it, but it's being tricky."

Then we receive a photo of one of the scientists holding the MINION aloft, just like Jackson did when the first one was retrieved here on R/V *Sarmiento de Gamboa*.

Ten minutes later we get another surprising message from RRS *Cook*. "Second blinking thing in sight. Identity TBD."

We wait.

Finally, a message. "Another MINION!"

Jackson is surprised because this MINION didn't call home when it returned to the surface. He thought it was lost forever. Getting it back will help engineers determine what went wrong and make improvements to the design.

The team on RRS *Cook* retrieves the second MINION. They'll later ship it back to the lab so engineers can remove the data and hopefully determine why it failed to signal its return.

SEARCHING FOR TZEX
May 18 (Day 20), 8:45 PM
THE PORCUPINE ABYSSAL PLAIN (PAP) • latitude 48.9° N, longitude 14.8° W

A little while ago, TZEX popped up to the surface after completing its programmed dive and pinged the team with its GPS coordinates. The captain motors the ship to the area, and everyone gathers at the starboard rail, scanning the water, seeking the flashing light. Jessica, Ken, and Elena are glad it came back up. (There's always a chance it won't.) Now we need to find it.

"There's a saying in oceanography: 'If you can't afford to lose it, don't put it over the side.' And that's literally what we're doing," says Ken. "We put this in the water not really knowing if it would come back. Or if it came back, if we could get to it quickly enough and get it safely out of the ocean without hitting it with the ship."

Finally someone on the bridge spots the light. The captain heads toward it and calls down to the bosun on deck. As we come up alongside TZEX, Ken, Jessica, and Elena stand ready to assist with recovery.

Despite the relatively calm seas, it still takes several tries to snag the yellow line attached to TZEX with a long-handled hook called a

CREW AND TECHNICIANS ON R/V SARMIENTO DE GAMBOA

The work of the science team isn't possible without the support of the ship's crew and marine technicians. All the crew and technicians are integral to ocean research. Most of the crew appears in the group photo on pages 116–117, but someone had to pilot the ship! And everyone is listed in the back of the book.

The crew works tirelessly to enable the science team's success. They are supposed to work in shifts, but that doesn't seem to matter. They are out on deck helping whenever needed. They weld pieces for the MOCNESS. They troubleshoot problems such as the twisted Stingray cable. They keep us well fed. And they help the captain make hard decisions about suspending over-the-side operations. Ultimately, they are the ones who look out for everyone's safety because they know the ship best and understand how it operates.

All of this happens between a Spanish-speaking crew and a primarily English-speaking science team.

At the end of the cruise Ken says, "We could communicate amongst each other, get things in and out of the water safely, and work together. That was really fun to see and very satisfying."

Despite language and culture differences, there is camaraderie among the crew and the scientists. Ken summarizes it best: "We left as strangers from the dock, but we came back as a family."

"pick pole" and feed the line to the crane. Then the bosun uses the winch to lift TZEX out of the water. Despite the taglines, TZEX still swings as the ship rolls. Elena and Jessica slide the cradle below it, and the team guides it into place.

"The physical process of removing something pretty small compared to the ship you're on is quite challenging," says Ken, "So when it gets back on board, there's a huge sigh of relief just for having accomplished that."

The primary goal of TZEX deployments was to test the engineering. The scientists wanted to see how well it would perform. Would it go to the appropriate depth, do its sampling, and return to the surface?

For the first deployment, they had trouble getting TZEX to go to the programmed depth and return. The up-and-down movement of TZEX is controlled by pushing oil into or out of a rubber bladder, which blows up like a balloon. Initially the motor didn't kick on and move oil into the bladder fast enough. On that first dive TZEX went too deep, hit neutral buoyancy for a while, and then came back up.

"It went lower than expected, but it did come back," says Jessica.

They had to find the sweet spot to get TZEX to work correctly. For this second dive, scientists changed the settings to move the oil sooner and pump it faster. This time TZEX worked much better.

"Before it was just dropping and dropping," says Jessica. "I was

Elena gets silly while waiting for a night recovery of TZEX.

It takes many people to deploy and recover TZEX.

worried it would keep going past its crush depth, which is 2,000 meters [about 1.25 miles]."

What's crush depth? That's the point where the equipment would implode from the pressure of the deep ocean. This explains everyone's joy upon recovery.

Ken says the deployment was "quite successful, even though in the short term it didn't produce a lot of data."

Ocean science is a long game. These important sea trials allow the team to get the engineering just right, which will result in lots of data in the future.

LAST BITS OF SCIENCE
May 19 (Day 21), 10:30 AM
THE PORCUPINE ABYSSAL PLAIN (PAP) • latitude 49.0° N, longitude 14.8° W

These last few days there's been a frenetic energy as scientists complete as many deployments and recoveries as possible before another storm rolls in and the ship must turn back toward Vigo. People aren't sleeping much, and the lab is busy 24/7. Among other things, there are three MOCNESS tows, five MINION deployments, three CTD casts, and multiple Stingray deployments, including one that lasts twelve hours. Marley and I go nonstop just like everyone else. We

Ken and Jessica are so excited, they kiss TZEX after it's safely recovered.

While Kayla is washing down nets, her PFD gets splashed and inflates.

shoot videos and photos to document as much as possible. We sleep in short bursts, sometimes going to bed at midnight and getting up again at three in the morning to document a MOCNESS recovery. Each time we lie down, Marley says, "Sleep fast!" which makes me laugh. We might still be sound asleep when our alarm goes off, but ten minutes later we're working on deck.

The team gets word that we must leave about eight hours earlier than planned. Heidi wants to leave the Stingray in longer, so she asks the captain for a little more time. His response is swift: we must leave now to beat the storm. We start our two-and-a-half-day journey back to Vigo.

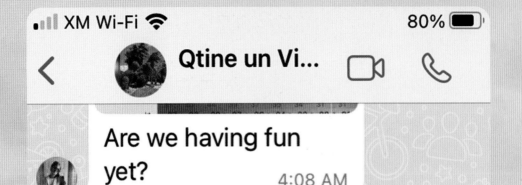
Are we having fun
yet?
4:08 AM

Nope. Sleeping is
impossible.
4:09 AM ✓✓

Erin E
that would explain the
broken glass & flying
around the lab   4:20 AM

to clarify the broken glass
was not from the lab, it
was in the mess
4:23 AM

Are you ok, Erin? I'm
obviously awake. I cou⌄
come and help you.
4:23 AM ✓✓

Late-night texting gets us through.

THE HOMESTRETCH

ANOTHER STORM?

May 20 (Day 22), 4:00 AM

THE NORTH ATLANTIC • *latitude 46.7° N, longitude 12.5° W*

WE TRY TO AVOID the worst of the storm, but it still catches up to us. I spend several hours in my bunk with my arms and legs spread out like a sea star, pressed against the sides of my bunk to brace myself and keep from falling out. Sleep is impossible, but there's nowhere better to go. As I search for my book in the darkness, Marley hears me moving around and exclaims, "Ugh!" She can't sleep either.

I turn on the light, clamber out of my lower bunk, sit on the extra bed, and face Marley as we talk. Our phones light up as Jessica sends a message. "Are we having fun yet?" She includes an image that makes us groan: a map of the weather system. It looks like a hurricane with its swirling wind patterns. We're in one heck of a storm.

More messages pop up as others join the conversation. Erin mentions being tossed around in the lab and broken glass in the mess. No one is sleeping.

I message: "I think this is the worst night yet."

Later my son tells me that he tracked the ship, and on this night we are in the windiest place on the planet. Some places, such as the tops of mountains, have stronger gusts during this time, but our location is consistently the windiest.

A couple hours later as breakfast nears, jokes start. Joel sends a group message: "Can we pay extra and get room service today?" Justin says he'll gladly deliver toast for fifty dollars. Jokes help get us through.

SHOWER SHUFFLE

I desperately want a shower after our last frenzied day of work, but now I question my decision as the ships rolls in the storm. I face the most challenging shower of the trip. I stare at the shower stall and contemplate my approach. I focus on the sensation of the waves, seeking a pattern. I step inside and make sure the door is closed tight. Then I wash up as quickly as possible while holding the grab bar with my left hand the whole time. I turn off the shower and watch the water slosh left to right with the rolls, waiting for it to drain enough for me to open the door. I step out, and a swell knocks me sideways into the sink. I decide to sit on the closed toilet to dry off and dress.

I open the door to our room as the ship rolls to port side. I skid across the room as the door bangs against the wall. It slams closed with the next wave. I sit on the edge of the bunk to pull on my socks and shoes. There's no way I can walk around in only socks. I need the grippy bottoms of my shoes to help keep me vertical.

Despite challenging conditions, I'm glad I had a shower. I feel refreshed and focused. It's like I washed my foggy brain down the drain. I sit at the desk and work on a final blog post. I'm here to write, and I'm responsible for working with Marley to produce daily posts about the expedition for the WHOI website. We have plenty to write about, but it's difficult to focus because of the weather. I'm glad to squeeze in a little work.

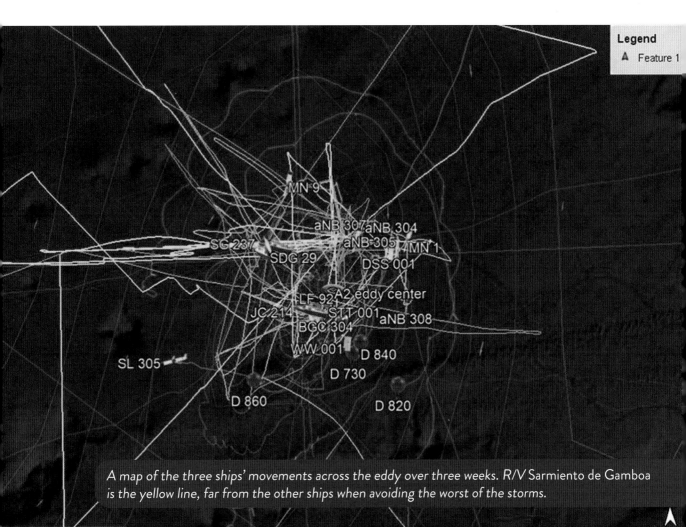

Legend
A Feature 1

MN 9
aNB 307 aNB 304
aNB 305 MN 1
SG 237
SDG 29   DSS 001
ILF 92 A2 eddy center
JC 214   STT 001
BGC 304   aNB 308
WW 001   D 840
SL 305
D 730
D 860   D 820

A map of the three ships' movements across the eddy over three weeks. R/V Sarmiento de Gamboa is the yellow line, far from the other ships when avoiding the worst of the storms.

Google Earth 0518   N

I'm on the stairs headed for the mess when I feel the ship rise up the wall of a giant wave. As we crest the wave, the stairs fall away. I feel weightless and my stomach bottoms out. I white-knuckle the railing, but it's not enough. My hand slides, and I'm tossed down a couple of steps before the ship slams into the base of the trough. Thankfully I don't fall. I make my way to the bottom as quickly as possible and take a couple deep breaths to calm myself.

Later that morning, Ken sends a message that doesn't surprise us: pinchos scheduled for two in the afternoon will move to Friday. He says, "I wonder why? And guess what? For the last time (I hope) I CAN say—the weather will only get better. . . ."

Indeed. We can only hope.

THE WEATHER DOES GET BETTER

Over the course of the day the weather does, in fact, gradually improve, but we're still pretty ragged and slow moving. It's been a harrowing three weeks with lots of storms, but there were also moments of incredible science, camaraderie, and learning.

"I love the challenge of studying the ocean and all of its incredible mysteries," says Heidi. "This expedition is especially fun and rewarding for me because I also like working with other people. The ocean is such a challenging place to understand; we need lots of diverse specializations and perspectives to hope to figure it out. To be able to work together with a big team is really exciting."

It will be years before scientists can fully analyze all the data collected on this expedition, but they already know that they were here at the right time to collect the kind of information they need.

 I ask Elena, "What's the most rewarding part of doing science at sea?" She says, "I think the relationships and the bonds you develop with people. That's amazing. It's like a family while you are on the ship. You discover people in a completely different way. You discover yourself as well. Being on a ship is isolating, you know, in the middle of the water. You have so much time to think from another perspective."

I understand this better now as we motor back toward Vigo. I'm glad the storms are over, and I'm also feeling a bit wistful. I know my time together with the scientists and crew is short.

On our last night at sea, we're rewarded with the most spectacular sunset of the entire trip. Someone says, "Red sky at night, sailor's delight." At least the rest of our journey back to Vigo will be smooth.

✺ DOLPHINS!
May 21 (Day 23), 10:30 AM
EN ROUTE TO VIGO

The lab bustles with activity. The laborious process of packing up has begun. The seas are calm, so scientists remove the ratchet straps and bungees and return equipment to bins and cases for shipping. It will be several hours before we reach Vigo, but everyone is eager to get as much done as possible so we can relax and blow off a little steam tonight.

Red sky at night, sailor's delight.

Dolphins!

But then someone calls out that there are dolphins off the starboard side. The lab empties as we gather at the rail with cameras and phones aimed at the water. People cheer as the dolphins jump.

"It's so amazing! Look at them!" exclaims Helena.

Henry says, "Ocean scientists act pretty serious until it's 'Dolphins on the starboard side!' and then everyone is screaming, me included."

After the long and arduous trip, the dolphins provide a joyous break in our day. They swim and leap alongside us for a long time, and we feel as if they are escorting us home.

Soon everyone is back at work deconstructing the lab and boxing up supplies. Heidi and John take down the cables between the lab and the winch while Justin disassembles the mass spectrometer. The hydro team secures water samples in padded boxes while Erin packs up the jumble of tubes and bottles. Meanwhile, the MOCNESS team hoses down the nets and spreads them out on the deck to dry.

🧭 PINCHOS AND GIFTS
2:00 PM

Today isn't Sunday, but Juan and Xoan prepare pinchos anyway to celebrate the end of our time at sea. The science team also brings gifts. We spread out WHOI T-shirts, hats, magnets, and stickers on a table. The crew and marine technicians choose from the items. The ship's crew and the science team mostly stood on opposite sides of the mess the first time we had pinchos together, but now we mingle and chat. A slide show of Marley's photos plays on a large screen. Marley shares an early draft of the video she's making about the cruise. We cheer and clap when it's done. Then we gather on the aft deck and take a group photo to commemorate this day.

LAND HO!
May 21, 6:00 PM
VIGO, SPAIN • *latitude 42.2° N, longitude 8.7° W*

I expect everyone to be excited and rush out on deck as land comes into view, but it's less dramatic. The science team has a lot of work to do before we reach Vigo, so they're pretty focused on their tasks. They know the shipping container arrives at the dock early tomorrow, and they need to have all their equipment ready to go. Even still, some people do stand at the rail as land grows closer. Once we're close to Vigo, eleven of us gather at the bow to celebrate our last bit of time on the water and watch Spain come into view.

Some of us gather at the bow as we enter Vigo, excited to be back.

Group photo.

Standing, back row, L–R (11 ppl):
Alejandro Buigues Diego, Santiago Riveira López, Joel Llopiz, Kayla Gardner, John San Soucie, Arturo Castellón Masalles, Rául Vicente Guillot Miralles, Xoan del Pozo Martínez, José Ignacio Fernández de Lera, Hector Sánchez Martínez, Alexi Shalapyonok

Standing, middle row, L–R (12 ppl):
Óscar Orizales Breijo, José Lino Baltasar Torres, Manuel Tomás Prego Castro, Jackson Sugar, Cristina García Fernández, Laetitia Drago, Helena McMonagle, Jessica Kozik, Manuel Domínguez Varo, Manuel Jerónimo de la Torre Cantero, Miguel Ángel Menéndez Pardiñas, David Liittschwager

Standing, front row, L–R (3 ppl):
José Llobet Peinador, Iván Domínguez Pouso, Ken Buesseler

Kneeling, back row, L–R (5 ppl):
Justin Ossolinski, Calixto Ponte Bermúdez, José Ignacio Domínguez Bouzada, Andres Giráldez Sotelo, Xoan Romero Lagoa

Kneeling, middle row: L–R (4 ppl):
Heidi Sosik, Julia Cox, Elena Ceballos Romero, Erin Frates

Sitting, front row, L–R (3 ppl):
Juan María Antelo Martínez, Michelle Cusolito, Henry Holm

Not pictured: Marley Parker, Alberto García Otero, Alejandro Barreiro Pereira, Román Miguel Palacios Vacas, Xoel Salgueiro McCormack

The ship is secured at the pier and packing and organizing continue. Bins and boxes are lined up on deck and placed inside giant crates or stacked on pallets and wrapped in plastic. The bosun hoists TZEX from its cradle and lowers it into a large wooden crate for shipping back to WHOI. The once-crammed lab feels spacious again.

Marley and I take a break and go for a walk. Due to Covid, we're not allowed to venture into the city, but the pier is behind a fence, and we can take walks inside the protected area. Stepping onto solid ground again feels momentous. As I walk up and down the length of the pier, my gait slowly returns to normal. We've walked with our legs wide apart for three weeks, so normal walking feels strange.

🧭 DEMOBILIZATION
May 22 (Day 24), 8:30 AM
VIGO, SPAIN • *latitude 42.2° N, longitude 8.7° W*

We start our day with the PCR Covid tests needed to return to each of our home countries. As soon as the shipping container arrives, the crew loads all the equipment inside it. The lab is busy, but the energy is different. The big energy of working at sea is replaced by a steady determination to finish packing. Everyone is glad to be back and looks forward to flying home to our loved ones, but a bit of sadness seems to hang in the air, too, as we face the fact that we have only one more day together.

Despite losing more than half the time to bad weather, the science team gathered a remarkable amount of data. How does Ken feel about the success of the mission?

He says the team was lucky. They had to choose the site carefully and decide what time of year to visit, but they were also at the mercy of the operators who decided when we could use the ship. Covid had

Me on the aft deck with Marley.

already caused a long delay, so he hadn't even been sure the expedition could get out this year.

"I'm pleased with the whole cruise," Ken says. "We got to the right place at the right time of the year."

The scientists wanted an area that was highly productive—where phytoplankton were growing fast and sucking in carbon dioxide—so they could study the fate of that carbon. And that's exactly what they found: an active spring bloom. Even though bad weather disrupted some scheduled deployments, the storms were spaced out, so sampling happened at the beginning, middle, and end of the cruise. That gives scientists what are called "time-series observations." They saw what happened to phytoplankton over time as they grew and then started to die off. The storms actually helped productivity by churning up the area and bringing in raw material, like nutrients from deeper waters, that plankton need to grow.

This phronima hollowed out a salp and moved inside.

Ken says, "It was early enough that the zooplankton—the animals that eat the phytoplankton—really hadn't reproduced fast enough to slow down or tamp down the phytoplankton's growth, so we had this really fast-growing bloom of plankton. They were forming what we call aggregates, or marine snow, attaching to each other and then sinking, presumably carrying a lot of material with them, including the carbon."

Many people ask what was discovered on this cruise. But science doesn't usually work like that. The millions of pieces of data collected during this expedition will help the team build a picture of how carbon moves through the ocean, but only after a ton of work back in the lab and office on shore. Those findings might inform international policy decisions related to global climate change. The data could also help governments write science-based regulations regarding how we use the ocean, such as in the fishing industry or for deep-sea mining.

The engineers and scientists on this team are part of the greater science community that investigates how the systems on our planet work. Building deep understanding takes time, and each new piece of information helps people make better decisions about how to use the resources on Earth.

As Heidi says, "Wouldn't it be amazing if we could make better decisions about how to manage the ocean twilight zone than we did with the surface waters?"

THE FUTURE OF OCEAN SCIENCE

Getting humans out onto the ocean to make firsthand observations is challenging. Expeditions are expensive, complicated, and use lots of resources. Ken says the future of ocean science lies in cutting-edge technologies like the ones deployed from

Strawberry squid look up with one eye and down with the other.

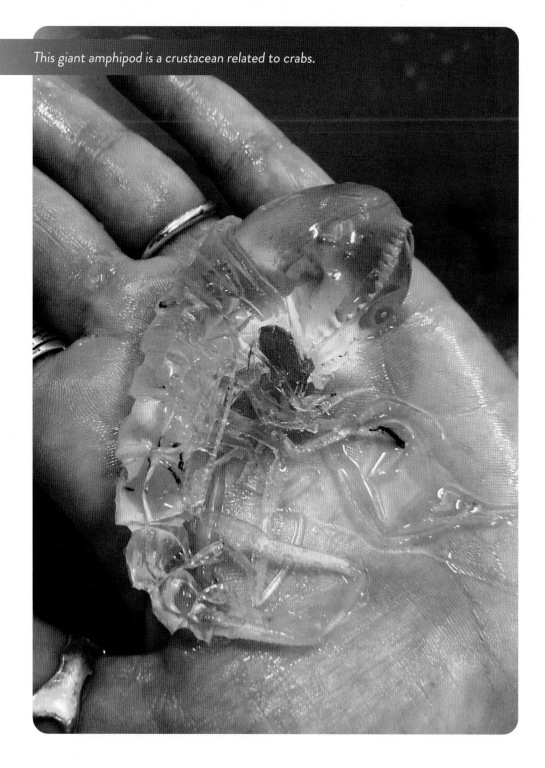

This giant amphipod is a crustacean related to crabs.

R/V *Sarmiento de Gamboa*. With a price tag of about 150,000 dollars, TZEX is an expensive piece of equipment, but as engineers perfect the technology and build more efficiently, costs will come down.

And then there are the small-but-mighty MINIONs. At about a thousand dollars each, they are far more affordable. Some people might feel discouraged that some MINIONs were lost during the expedition, but that's all part of the design and engineering process. Of course the team wishes all the MINIONs had been recovered, but they learned a lot from the deployments and can now make improvements.

"Doing low-cost science comes with a particular set of compromises," Jackson says. "But successfully completing a mission and proving that this technology works is exciting for the future of oceanography."

MINIONs will be fine-tuned until they consistently work well. Then a network of MINIONs and other autonomous devices will collect data from all over the world, and various underwater networks can convey data back to land via satellite.

Because MINIONs are small, they can be deployed off any vessel: a sailboat or tour boat could put one over the side. Over time, more and more new underwater robots such as TZEX and MINIONs will collect data and send it back to scientists on shore.

"I don't think we're going to get there tomorrow," says Ken. "But maybe next time, instead of three ships and a few robots, we'll have one ship and hundreds of robots. We're going to move toward systems that collect data more autonomously."

This expedition helped scientists get one step closer to that reality.

Aerial view of WHOI's docks in Woods Hole, Massachusetts, on Cape Cod.

EPILOGUE 4 DAYS LATER **&** 1 YEAR LATER

ADJUSTING

May 26 (4 days after the end of the voyage)
WHOI, Falmouth, Massachusetts, United States
latitude 41.5° N, longitude 70.7° W

NOW THAT WE'RE HOME, we check in and discover that many of us find adjusting to regular life challenging. Our time at sea was often harrowing, and yet we miss it. Why? Many people love the excitement of being at sea—the adventure of it. For others the possibility of seeing or discovering something new drives them. Many of us miss the camaraderie of living and working together in intense conditions. We came to depend on one another in a way that doesn't usually happen in everyday life. We got to see one another at our best when we completed difficult tasks or solved problems together. And we saw one another struggle due to lack of sleep, days of seasickness, or anxiety about raging storms.

As Helena says, "The bonding is unique. Part of that is you see each other when you're vulnerable: when you're seasick, or really tired, or you lose your equipment to the bottom of the ocean and you can't get it back. Or you miss someone back on shore. All of these things bring us together because we're literally in the same boat."

Deep bonds are formed during such conditions. We relied on one another for so much, and we know we can't maintain the exact bonds and relationships that existed on the R/V *Sarmiento de Gamboa*. Even if some members of the group go to sea again, it will be with different people on a different ship in different conditions. Perhaps a bitter-sweet quality makes us miss being at sea: we can never have the exact experience again, but many of us will keep chasing it.

We're also thankful we had the opportunity to experience life and work at sea in the first place. "In this day and age, people don't really travel by ship anymore—they usually fly or drive," says John. "So to be at sea at all is a rare gift. But to get to see the creatures that inhabit the ocean in the way that scientists on a research vessel do, it's an extraor-dinary perspective and an incredibly valuable one. I feel very lucky to get a glimpse into something that is so mysterious."

 ## EARLY RESULTS

The Next May (1 year after the end of the voyage)
WHOI, FALMOUTH, MASSACHUSETTS, UNITED STATES
latitude 41.5° N, longitude 70.7° W

One year after the end of the expedition, scientists have been able to draw some early conclusions. It's important to note that these are not due solely to the data gathered on R/V *Sarmiento de Gamboa*. Every new insight builds on previous research. Scientists on this expedition also collaborated with scientists from other research institutions to compare their data and results.

Here are a few findings of the Ocean Twilight Zone Project so far:

- Certain fish, such as bristlemouths and lanternfish, seem to prefer specific kinds of prey rather than eating what's avail-able. Some other fish eat whatever they can find.
- Mesopelagic fish respiration rates measured on R/V *Sarmiento de Gamboa* are similar to measurements collected in the

1980s. When scientists use multiple methods over time and see similar results, they gain confidence in those results. In addition, the more precisely scientists can estimate fish respiration, the more precisely they can describe how much carbon fish move from the surface to the deep ocean.

- Invertebrates might migrate at different rates depending on the amount of light at the ocean surface. Things like cloud cover during the day and the level of moonlight at night may influence migration.

- eDNA stays at about the same depth after it's shed by an animal rather than sinking deeper or rising into shallower waters. This means scientists can determine the depth where those animals lived, which provides valuable information about diel vertical migration.

- Top predators such as swordfish, seals, sharks, and whales dive to the twilight zone to eat more frequently than was previously thought. Even though they spend much of their lives near the surface, the deep ocean is important for their survival.

Scientists will process samples, analyze data, and draw conclusions for many years. They'll also design new experiments to seek answers to questions that arise as they discover more.

Before we even departed Vigo, Ken said, "Every time we go out to sea we learn something. It might not be an ah-ha moment. It might come two years later after I've analyzed what I found against what someone else found. Often we're putting these puzzles together over many years. It's a puzzle you put together by getting all the parts: from the biology to the chemistry to the physical properties of the water and how those interact with each other. That's the real mystery."

To dive deeper into the twilight zone and to see the most up-to-date news, visit **https://twilightzone.whoi.edu**. Go into the deep unknown!

MORE INFORMATION

DETAILS ABOUT THE VOYAGE

Brief passages in this book were first published on the WHOI "Dive and Discover" website in slightly different form in blog posts written by author Michelle Cusolito. Those passages are used here with permission.

WHOI's Ocean Twilight Zone project is fully funded by the Audacious Project, housed at TED. Members of the OTZ team sailed on *R/V Sarmiento de Gamboa* in partnership with the NASA-funded EXPORTS mission.

"By the Numbers" was compiled and written by Marley Parker and Michelle Cusolito, and a version of it originally appeared on "Dive and Discover." It's printed here with permission from both Marley and WHOI.

A NOTE ABOUT TIME

The ship went through three different time zones during the expedition.

In Vigo, Spain, the time is UTC +2. ("Universal Time Coordinated" plus two hours. UTC is a standard used throughout the world to regulate time.) In order to coordinate with the other two ships, which departed from the United Kingdom, the ships all adjusted onto the same time zone. The ships agreed to operate on UTC. In order to get on UTC, R/V *Sarmiento de Gamboa* moved our clocks back one hour the first night at sea and another hour the second night at sea. Then on the return trip to Vigo, we reversed it and added one hour the first night and another hour the second night.

In addition, the ship operates on a twenty-four-hour clock (often called military time in the United States). So 1:00 PM is 1300, 2:00 PM is 1400, etc.

To prevent confusion, whenever I mention time in this book, I use the current time on the ship and designate morning (AM) and night (PM) when necessary. I also rounded some of the times to the nearest quarter hour to simplify things.

✦ TIPS FOR KIDS WHO WANT TO BE AN OCEANOGRAPHER OR A MARINE SCIENTIST

Any curious person can be a great scientist. Believe in yourself and follow your interests.

- Work hard at school. You don't need straight As, but you should do your best and take advantage of available opportunities.
- Learn as much math as you can during high school, college, and graduate school. Every good scientist uses math in their work.
- Work on your communication skills. Scientists write papers and grants and communicate with the public.
- Seek out opportunities to meet and connect with scientists who work in the field you want to study. For example, WHOI offers a variety of educational events that are open to the public. Lots of science museums, aquariums, and research institutions do the same. Once you get to high school and college, apply for internships with scientists.

⊕ BY THE NUMBERS

A lot happened during three action-packed weeks aboard the R/V *Sarmiento de Gamboa*.

A quick overview of the expedition:
- 14 days of pre-expedition quarantine
- 8 tons of equipment transported from Woods Hole, Massachusetts, to Vigo, Spain
- 19 science team members on board
- 24 crew and marine technicians
- 24 days on the vessel
- Approximately 1,900 nautical miles traveled

A few numbers about the science operations:
- 2,000 meters (1.25 miles) of depth reached by deployed equipment
- 782 hours of continuous underway water sampling
- 9 MINIONs deployed (4 MINIONs recovered)
- 3 TZEX deployments and recoveries
- 600 liters (158.5 gallons) of water imaged by TZEX
- 9 MOCNESS tows
- 78,411,000 liters (20,713,994 gallons) of water sampled by the MOCNESS
- 12 CTD rosette casts
- 2,880 liters (761 gallons) of water collected by the CTD rosette
- 11 Stingray deployments
- 7 million liters (1.85 million gallons) of water imaged by the Stingray sled
- 3,024,000 images captured by the Stingray sled
- 323,000 images from one Underwater Vision Profiler (UVP)
- 10,500 images from the PlanktoScope
- 4,470,000 images from the Imaging FlowCytobot (IFCB)

During this expedition we consumed lots of food:
- 90 eggs in just one meal (so many on the whole trip!)
- 500 loaves of bread (more than half a loaf per person per day!)
- 3,000 cups of espresso/cappuccino
- 9 kilograms (20 pounds) of jamón (Spanish dry-cured ham)
- 4 meals of traditional pinchos (small snacks)
- 500 kilograms (1,102 pounds) of food overall

A few numbers about life on board:
- 6 nations represented (United States, Spain, United Kingdom, France, Belarus, Canada)
- 83 Styrofoam cups shrunk during CTD casts for souvenirs
- 200 hours of sustained winds over 20 knots
- 11 Life Savers candies used for science
- 313 Life Savers candies consumed by the science team (ha!)
- 1,744 WhatsApp messages exchanged among science team members
- 5 on-ship bike rides completed by Joel Llopiz
- 4,472 photos taken by the onboard communications team (Marley and Michelle)

And finally here are a few things we can't quite calculate numbers for:
- the number of times food trays slid off tables during meals
- the number of squats done during group workouts
- the number of mystery bruises acquired from bumping into walls, doors, railings, and equipment
- the number of times Ken said, "The weather will only get better."

⊛ CRUISE PARTICIPANTS

Lead Investigators

Ken Buesseler, co-chief scientist, WHOI

Heidi Sosik, co-chief scientist, WHOI

Joel Llopiz, biologist, WHOI

Graduate Students and Postdocs

Cristina García Fernández, PhD student, Institute of Marine Research (IIM-CSIC), Spain

Elena Ceballos Romero, postdoctoral investigator, WHOI Buesseler Lab

Helena McMonagle, graduate student, University of Washington

Henry Holm, PhD student, MIT-WHOI joint program

John San Soucie, PhD student, MIT-WHOI joint program

Kayla Gardner, PhD student, MIT-WHOI joint program

Laetitia Drago, PhD student, IMEV lab, Villefranche-sur-Mer, France

Scientists and Engineers

Alexi Shalapyonok, research associate III, WHOI Sosik Lab

Erin Frates, research assistant, WHOI Govindarajan Lab

Jackson Sugar, associate engineer, Omand Lab, University of Rhode Island

Jessica Kozik, research assistant, WHOI Buesseler Lab

Julia Cox, research assistant, WHOI Llopiz Lab

Justin Ossolinski, senior research assistant, WHOI Stanley Lab, Wellesley College

Communications

Marley Parker, videographer, photographer, and science writer

Michelle Cusolito, author, educator, and science communicator

David Liittschwager, *National Geographic* photographer

✸ CREW AND MARINE TECHNICIANS ON R/V SARMIENTO DE GAMBOA

Named in the text

Juan María Antelo Martínez, first cook

Xoan del Pozo Martínez, cook's assistant

Not named in the text

Alberto García Otero, second officer

Alejandro Barreiro Pereira, oiler

Alejandro Buigues Diego, captain in training

Andres Giráldez Sotelo, marine technician

Arturo Castellón Masalles, chief technician

Calixto Ponte Bermúdez, chief mechanic

Hector Sánchez Martínez, marine technician

Iván Domínguez Pouso, seaman

José Ignacio Domínguez Bouzada, seaman

José Ignacio Fernández de Lera, electro-technical officer

José Lino Baltasar Torres, seaman

José Llobet Peinador, first mechanic officer

Manuel Domínguez Varo, seaman

Manuel Jerónimo de la Torre Cantero, seaman

Manuel Tomás Prego Castro, oiler

Miguel Ángel Menéndez Pardiñas, captain

Óscar Orizales Breijo, bosun

Rául Vicente Guillot Miralles, marine technician

Román Miguel Palacios Vacas, oiler

Santiago Riveira López, first officer

Xoel Salgueiro McCormack, captain in training

Xoan Romero Lagoa, marine technician

🧭 ABOUT QUOTES, SOURCES, AND EXPERTS

I based the main narrative on my experiences during quarantine in Vigo, Spain, from April 15, 2021, to April 29, 2021, and on board R/V *Sarmiento de Gamboa* from April 29, 2021, to May 23, 2021. Along with Marley Parker, I recorded details of life on the ship and conducted interviews with the researchers, both via Zoom while in quarantine and in person while on board. I also pulled details from our WhatsApp chats and the official scientific logs. When I couldn't remember a detail, I consulted the thousands of photos and videos that Marley and I took. In addition, I verified details with people in follow-up interviews and via email or WhatsApp after the voyage. Unless otherwise noted, all quotations are from notes, videos, or WhatsApp chats. I occasionally edited a quotation slightly for clarity, and all edits were approved by the speaker. Everyone from the science team on board the R/V *Sarmiento de Gamboa* read and approved the sections where they were quoted or when I talked about their work. Additionally the entire manuscript was read by Kathryn Baltes, Phil Renaud, Heidi Sosik, Joel Llopiz, Helena McMonagle, and Marley Parker. Two scientists who were not on board also suggested important edits: Annette Govindarajan is the lead scientist for the eDNA component of the Ocean Twilight Zone Project, and Melissa Omand is the lead scientist and developer of MINIONs.

In addition to the scientists and engineers on the expedition, I also talked to the following WHOI scientists, engineers, and marine policy experts: Simon Thorrold, Andone Lavery, Larry Madin, Paul Caiger, Annette Govindarajan, Helen Fredricks, Dana Yoerger, Porter Hoagland, and Di Jin. I also made use of numerous books and other sources, some of which are listed in the bibliography, to better understand the technicalities of the work.

SOURCES

BOOKS AND ARTICLES

Berwald, Juli. *Spineless: The Science of Jellyfish and the Art of Growing a Backbone.* New York: Riverhead Books, 2017.

Courage, Katherine Harmon. *Octopus! The Most Mysterious Creature in the Sea.* New York: Current, 2013.

Gershwin, Lisa-Ann. *Jellyfish: A Natural History.* Chicago: University of Chicago Press, 2016.

Hadfield, Chris. *An Astronaut's Guide to Life on Earth: What Going to Space Taught Me About Ingenuity, Determination, and Being Prepared for Anything.* New York: Little, Brown and Company, 2013.

Hanlon, R., et al. *Octopus, Squid, and Cuttlefish: A Visual, Scientific Guide to the Oceans' Most Advanced Invertebrates.* Chicago: University of Chicago Press, 2018.

Hoyt, Erich. *Creatures of the Deep: In Search of the Sea's "Monsters" and the World They Live In.* Richmond Hill, Ontario: Firefly Books, 2021.

Johnsen, S., et al. "Propagation and Perception of Bioluminescence: Factors Affecting Counterillumination as a Cryptic Strategy." *Biological Bulletin,* 207, no. 1 (2004): 1–16. doi:10.2307/1543624.

Kirby, Richard R. *Ocean Drifters: A Secret World Beneath the Waves.* Buffalo, NY: Firefly Books, 2010.

Knowlton, Nancy. *Citizens of the Sea: Wondrous Creatures from the Census of Marine Life.* Washington, DC: National Geographic, 2010.

Lee, G., and Jamie Stokes. *Marine Science: An Illustrated Guide to Science.* New York: Chelsea House, 2006.

Montgomery, Sy. *The Soul of an Octopus: A Surprising Exploration into the Wonder of Consciousness.* New York: Atria Books, 2016.

Nouvian, Claire. *The Deep: The Extraordinary Creatures of the Abyss.* Chicago: University of Chicago Press, 2007.

Paul, J., et al. "In Situ Instrumentation." *Oceanography,* 20, no. 2 (2007): 70–78. www.jstor.org/stable/24860045.

Priede, Imants G. *Deep-Sea Fishes: Biology, Diversity, Ecology and Fisheries.* Cambridge, England: Cambridge University Press, 2017.

Robison, B., et al. "The Coevolution of Midwater Research and ROV Technology at MBARI." *Oceanography,* 30, no. 4 (2017): 26–37. www.jstor.org/stable/26367623.

Scales, Helen. *The Brilliant Abyss: Exploring the Majestic Hidden Life of the Deep Ocean and the Looming Threat That Imperils It.* New York: Atlantic Monthly Press, 2021.

Streever, Bill. *In Oceans Deep: Courage, Innovation, and Adventure Beneath the Waves.* New York: Little, Brown and Company, 2019.

Widder, Edith. *Below the Edge of Darkness: A Memoir of Exploring Light and Life in the Deep Sea.* New York: Random House, 2021.

Woods Hole Oceanographic Institution. "Ocean Twilight Zone Project Annual Report." Woods Hole Oceanographic Institution's Ocean Twilight Zone Project, June 1, 2022.

Woods Hole Oceanographic Institution. *Oceanus: The Journal of Our Ocean Planet: Ocean Twilight Zone: Exploring a Hidden Frontier.* 54, no 1 (2019). www.whoi.edu/oceanus.

WEBSITES

Dive and Discover: Into the Twilight Zone. https://divediscover.whoi.edu/expedition17
    Website focused on this particular expedition

Encyclopedia of Life. https://eol.org/
    Global access to knowledge about life on Earth

Monterey Bay Aquarium Research Institute. https://www.mbari.org/
    A nonprofit oceanographic research center

Ocean Biogeographic Information Systems. https://obis.org/
    Global open-access data and information clearinghouse on marine biodiversity for science,
    conservation, and sustainable development

Ocean Twilight Zone. https://twilightzone.whoi.edu/
    Information and updates regarding Ocean Twilight Zone research

World Register of Marine Species. http://www.marinespecies.org/index.php
    An authoritative classification and catalogue of marine names

PODCASTS

Catch Our Drift. https://catchourdrift.org/

Kathy Sullivan Explores. https://www.kathysullivanexplores.com/podcast

Ocean Science Radio. https://oceanscienceradio.simplecast.com/

Proceedings of the National Academy of Sciences, Science Sessions.
    https://www.pnas.org/page/media/podcasts

How to Protect the Ocean. https://www.speakupforblue.com/show/speak-up-for-the-ocean-blue/

LEARN MORE

You can learn more about the expedition featured in this book and about Woods Hole Oceanographic Institution's work by exploring their website. I recommend the following specific pages:

- About the Ocean Twilight Zone generally: https://twilightzone.whoi.edu
- About this expedition: https://divediscover.whoi.edu/expedition17
- To see a variety of interactive animations that explain the carbon cycle, migration, etc.:
  https://divediscover.whoi.edu/ocean-twilight-zone-infomod
- To see images from the Imaging FlowCytobot (IFCB) and learn more about how it works (click
  to see images of the bins from the expedition in this book):
  https://ifcb-data.whoi.edu/timeline?dataset=OTZ_Atlantic&cruise=SG2105

EVEN MORE

For videos from this expedition, visit **www.michellecusolito.com/wotz** or scan the QR code here.

I encourage you to do research of your own, too. For example, there is great info about the biological carbon pump if you search on YouTube. What terms from the book can you search online to find out more? What books can you find to learn more about the ocean?

Dive deep!

⊕ ACKNOWLEDGMENTS

I extend my deepest gratitude to my shipmates. I'll never forget our time together. Thank you, WHOI and all the experts I consulted. Special thanks to Ken Buesseler, Heidi Sosik, and Joel Llopiz, who took a chance and invited a children's book author to participate in this extraordinary expedition. Thanks to Joanne Tromp for first connecting me to the OTZ team, and to Kathryn Baltes, Phil Renaud, and Ken Kostel for championing this project from the beginning. Thanks to Natalie Renier for the gorgeous endpaper maps.

Thank you to my editor Karen Boss, for making me a better writer. I adore working with you. Thanks to Charlesbridge Creative Director Diane Earley for taking my vision and making it a work of art, and to the entire team, including Alyssa Mito Pusey, Betsy Uhrig, Jackie Dever, Donna Spurlock, Jordan Standridge, and Megan Quinn for everything from text notes to copyediting to proofreading to sales to marketing magic. A special thank you to Eight Cousins Books in Falmouth, Massachusetts, for your unwavering support.

I'm grateful for so many people in my life. Here are some of them:

The "Lipstick Gals," my ironically named nonfiction crew: Loree Griffin Burns, Sarah Albee, Karen Romano Young, Pamela Courtney, and M. O. Yuksel. You kept me writing through the pandemic.

My critique group: Kristy Acevedo, Peter Arenstam, and Nichole Charbonneau. Our group has been my consistent and steady support for fifteen-plus years. I would not survive in this business without you.

My agent James McGowan: staunch advocate, enthusiastic cheerleader, and hilarious friend. Working with you is a joy.

Mom and Dad: This kid from a small town would never have gone on an expedition like this if you hadn't encouraged me to be a high-school exchange student to the Philippines. That year altered the course of my life and showed me I could do adventurous things.

My mother-in-law, Ellie, my unofficial head of sales: Tell her you want to purchase a book—she'll make sure you don't forget. She also knows about going to sea.

My father-in-law, Richard: this was my last book he knew about, and I wish he could see the final product.

My inner circle: Monique, Don, Luca, Evo, Melissa, Isaac, Zoe, Zeke, Kimberly and Ben, Christina, Bryan, Ethan, Tanner, Alison, Andrea and Mark, Kristin and Duane, Lisa, Aravind, Anya, and Otha.

My kids, Dante and Alia: You inspire me. The world is so much better because you're in it.

Rick, my one and only: I am profoundly grateful we found each other all those years ago. You make living this life wonderful.

And finally, all the readers of my books: you're the reason I write.

⊛ IMAGE CREDITS

Front cover: Top: © Woods Hole Oceanographic Institution (WHOI), Paul Caiger; Right: © WHOI, Marley Parker; Bottom: © WHOI, Marley Parker

Back cover: © WHOI, Marley Parker

Endpapers: © WHOI, Natalie Renier

Title page: © WHOI, Marley Parker

Prologue: opposite p. 1: Michelle Cusolito

Chapter 1: p. 4: Michelle Cusolito; p. 5 © WHOI, Marley Parker; pp. 8-9: © WHOI, Marley Parker; p. 11: © WHOI, Paul Caiger; p. 13: Michelle Cusolito; p. 14: Michelle Cusolito; p. 16: © WHOI, Marley Parker; p. 17: © WHOI, Marley Parker

Chapter 2: p. 18: Michelle Cusolito; p. 21: © WHOI, Marley Parker; p. 22: © WHOI, Julia Cox; p. 25: © WHOI, Marley Parker; p. 26: © WHOI, Marley Parker; p. 27: © WHOI, Marley Parker; pp. 28-29: © WHOI, Natalie Renier; p. 31: © WHOI, Marley Parker

Chapter 3: p. 32: © WHOI, Marley Parker; p. 35: © WHOI, Marley Parker; p. 36: Michelle Cusolito; p. 39: Michelle Cusolito; p. 41: Michelle Cusolito; p. 42: Michelle Cusolito; p. 43: © WHOI, Marley Parker; p. 44: © WHOI, Marley Parker; p. 45: © WHOI, Marley Parker

Chapter 4: p. 46: Michelle Cusolito; p. 49: Michelle Cusolito; p. 50: © WHOI; p. 51: © WHOI; p. 53: © WHOI, Marley Parker; p. 56: © WHOI, Marley Parker; p. 58: Michelle Cusolito

Chapter 5: p. 60: © WHOI, Justin Ossolinski; p. 62: Michelle Cusolito; p. 64: © WHOI, Joel Llopiz (still shot of a video); p. 68: © WHOI, Marley Parker

Chapter 6: p. 70: © WHOI, Marley Parker; p. 72: © WHOI, Marley Parker; p. 73 © WHOI, Marley Parker; p. 74: © WHOI, Marley Parker; p. 75: © WHOI, Joel Llopiz; p. 77: © WHOI, Marley Parker; p. 78: © WHOI, Marley Parker; p. 79: © WHOI, Marley Parker; p. 80: © WHOI, Marley Parker; p. 81 © WHOI, Marley Parker; pp. 82-83: © WHOI, Natalie Renier; p. 85: © WHOI, Marley Parker; p. 87: Michelle Cusolito/Laetitia Drago; p. 88: © WHOI, Marley Parker

Chapter 7: p. 90: © WHOI, Marley Parker; p. 93: © WHOI, Marley Parker; p. 94: © WHOI, Marley Parker; p. 96: © WHOI, Marley Parker; p. 97: Michelle Cusolito

Chapter 8: p. 98: © WHOI, Marley Parker; p. 104: © WHOI, Marley Parker; p. 105: Michelle Cusolito; p. 106: © WHOI, Marley Parker; p. 107: © WHOI, Marley Parker

Chapter 9: p. 108: Michelle Cusolito (screenshot); p. 111: © WHOI; p. 113: Michelle Cusolito; p. 114: Michelle Cusolito; p. 115: © WHOI, Marley Parker; p. 116-117: © WHOI, Marley Parker; p. 119: © WHOI; p. 120: © WHOI, Paul Caiger; p. 121: Michelle Cusolito; p. 122: Michelle Cusolito

Epilogue: p. 124: © WHOI

 ## INDEX

Page numbers in *italics* indicate illustrations.

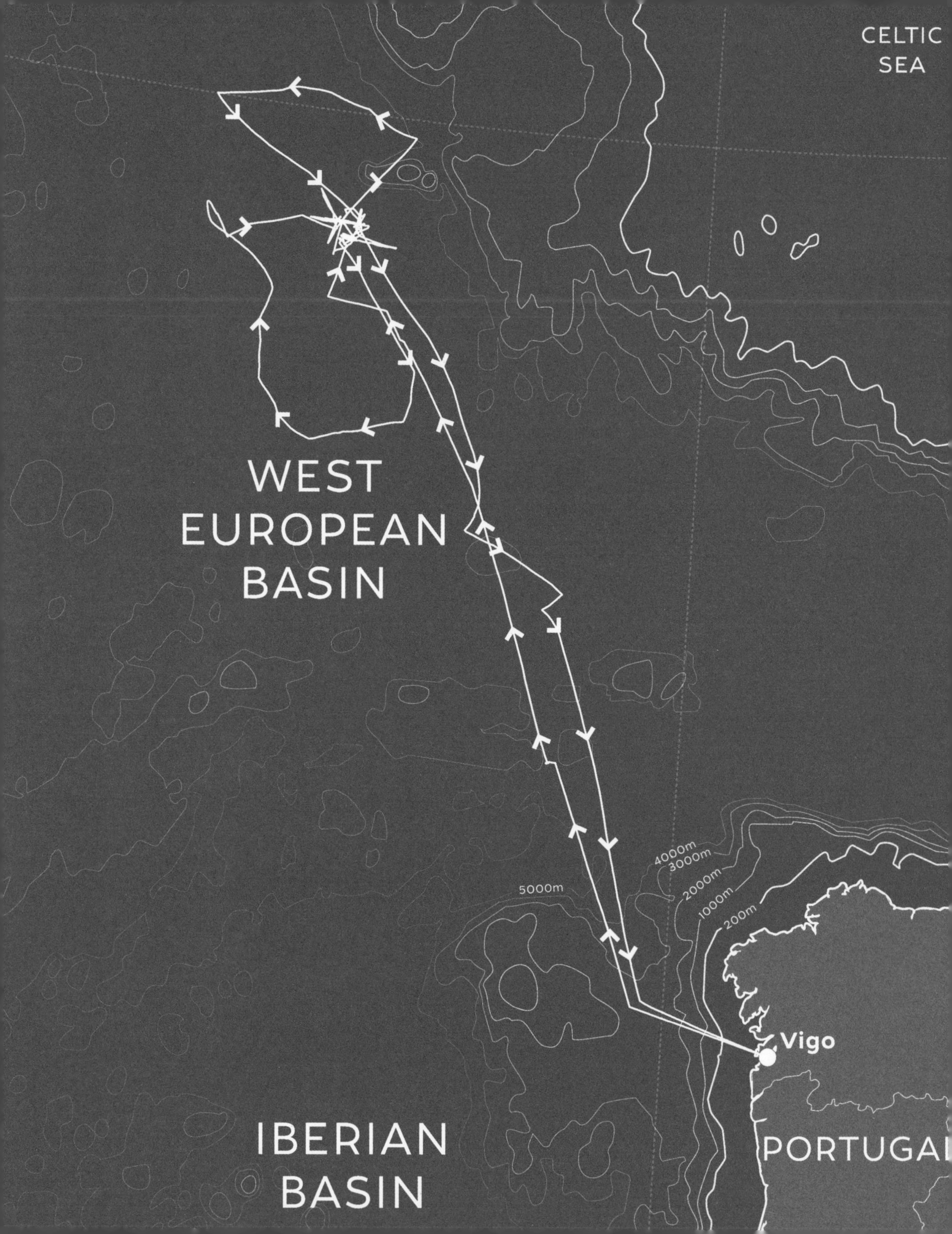

CELTIC
SEA

WEST
EUROPEAN
BASIN

IBERIAN
BASIN

PORTUGAL

Vigo

5000m

4000m
3000m
2000m
1000m
200m